THE WORK
OF THE
BIVOCATIONAL
MINISTER

THE WORK OF THE BIVOCATIONAL MINISTER

DENNIS W. BICKERS

JUDSON PRESS
PUBLISHERS SINCE 1824
VALLEY FORGE

THE WORK OF THE BIVOCATIONAL MINISTER

© 2007 by Judson Press, Valley Forge, PA 19482-0851

Library of Congress Cataloging-in-Publication Data

Bickers, Dennis W., 1948-
The work of the bivocational minister / Dennis W. Bickers.
p. cm.
ISBN-13: 978-0-8170-1510-7 (pbk. : alk. paper) 1. Clergy—Secular employment. I. Title. BV676.5.B54 2007
253'.2—dc22   2006034760

Printed on recycled paper in the U.S.A.

First Printing, 2007.

DEDICATION

Since 2000 I have had the opportunity to work as an area
resource minister with the American Baptist Churches of Indiana
and Kentucky. Working with these dedicated men and women as
we serve the churches in our region has been a joy. Each member of our staff believes in bivocational ministry and continually
seeks opportunities to recognize and honor individuals and
churches who have been led to this form of ministry. I am proud
to dedicate this book to the members of our region staff: Dan
Barringer, Dan Cash, Bethany Dunaway, Phyllis Goodyear,
Mary Kassel, Larry Mason, Don Scott, Anita Sipe, Jim Walter,
and Mike Wilson.

May God continue to bless each of you and your families.

CONTENTS

CONCLUSION

APPENDIXES

INTRODUCTION

In 1981 I sat before the pastoral search committee of Hebron Baptist Church, a small rural church near my hometown of Madison, Indiana. They had been seeking a pastor for more than a year without success. The church had an aging, dwindling congregation and had significant financial difficulties. The primary question the committee had for me was whether I thought their church had any hope of survival. I had already filled the pulpit on three occasions, and after our meeting the committee asked if I would be willing to preach a trial sermon the following Sunday. After that sermon the church unanimously voted to call me as their next pastor.

My wife and I went home excited about the prospect of leading my first church. Although I had no experience and no education beyond high school, I knew God had called me to pastor a church, and this congregation seemed to be a good fit. It wasn't until later that night, after I had gone to bed, that the reality of the day hit me. I sat up as the thought went through my mind, *Now that I have them, what am I going to do with them?* My excitement quickly turned to concern as I realized I really didn't know how to lead a church. That night I spent more time in prayer than in sleep.

Twenty years later I resigned from that church to accept the position of area minister with the American Baptist Churches of Indiana and Kentucky. The church and I grew a lot during those two decades. We learned much about grace and hope and experienced many exciting victories and a few disappointments.

We also learned about the benefits and challenges of bivocational ministry. During my entire ministry at Hebron I was bivocational. For most of that time, I worked in a factory on an assembly line and various machine lines. During my last two years at the church, I was able to take early retirement from the factory, but just prior to doing so, our family took ownership of a heating and air-conditioning business, which I continue to manage today. While serving this church, I also graduated from a nearby Bible college and later earned a bachelor's degree. Because I was bivocational, the church grew to understand that ministry belonged to all the members of the church, and we learned how better to work together to accomplish the ministry God had given us.

Measuring Successful Bivocational Ministry

Successful ministry is often determined by measuring the numerical growth of the membership, the number of baptisms each year, financial income, or the new buildings built. If bivocational ministers measure the success of their ministries by such accounting methods, few will feel very successful. There are many reasons numerical growth may be difficult in a church—reasons that have nothing to do with having a bivocational minister. That does not mean, however, that significant ministry is not occurring in that church.

Pat Lanman is the editor of a local newspaper and the bivocational pastor of Olive Branch Baptist Church in southeastern Indiana. This church is located in a rather isolated, rural area that does not lend itself to hosting a megachurch. Although the church has seen some solid numerical growth since Lanman became the pastor, its more significant ministry occurs several hundreds of miles away in the Appalachian area of southeastern Kentucky. Two years ago the church members determined they wanted to have more missionary involvement than merely giving money to the denominational mission offerings. They felt led to begin a ministry in Appalachia but were not sure how to begin. Lanman contacted me, and I suggested he speak to another pastor whose church already had a ministry in that region. This other pastor introduced Lanman to a ministry in that area, and the church soon began assisting that local ministry.

Olive Branch has taken school supplies, clothing, and food to the region to distribute to persons needing assistance. Now they have involved other churches in their association, and last year I joined about fourteen men from their association who went down to this area to begin winterizing houses. This is a ministry that will not lead to any measurable growth in Olive Branch's church, but it should be considered a successful ministry.

The Call to Bivocational Ministry

The call to bivocational ministry is no less valid than the call to a fully funded ministry. It is simply a call to a different type of ministry that is needed by many of our churches today. Research has shown that many ministers are reluctant to serve in smaller churches, and finding pastors for these congregations is becoming increasingly more difficult.[1] God is not surprised by this statistic, and the Holy Spirit is responding by calling many men and women to meet the ministry needs in these faith communities. Many have heard this call and are now serving as bivocational ministers. This book is written to encourage those who are serving faithfully in a bivocational leadership role. It is also written for those who are considering such a call, because the need for bivocational ministers is great and will continue to grow. Churches need your leadership if they are to fulfill God's vision for their ministries. From personal experience I can assure you that it will be a rewarding ministry that will bring great blessings to you and to the people you serve.

Structure of the Book

In chapter 1 I define bivocational ministry and examine how it has been perceived in recent years. Unfortunately, not everyone sees bivocational ministry as a positive option for churches, and we will try to understand why that viewpoint exists.

Chapter 2 looks at the biblical and historical precedents for bivocational ministry. In this chapter we will find that the tentmaking minister has a much longer history than the fully funded minister.

Chapter 3 provides a profile of the typical bivocational minister. Much of the data in this chapter comes from a limited study I did in 2004 of bivocational ministers in the American Baptist Churches USA. Regrettably, little updated or more comprehensive data seems to be available in this area.

In chapter 4 I identify places where bivocational ministry is found. Bivocational ministry is not just happening in small, struggling churches; it can be found in new church plants, larger church settings, and multistaff churches.

We will study some of the risks associated with bivocational ministry in chapter 5. Bivocational ministry has many of the same risks as fully funded ministry, but it also has some unique challenges.

Chapter 6 looks at the other side of that coin: the rewards of being bivocational. These rewards exist for both the minister and the church being served, and they far outnumber the challenges and difficulties.

We will try to examine a typical week in the life of a bivocational minister in chapter 7. I say "try" because every bivocational minister is different with a different schedule and range of responsibilities outside the church. This is a key chapter because it also looks at the need to balance all the commitments the bivocational minister has in his or her life.

In the final chapter we will see how bivocational ministry is being embraced by different denominations and by the emerging church. One of the interesting aspects of bivocational ministry is that many denominations are now recognizing its importance but are not sure how to support it within their structures.

At the end of most chapters, I recommend resources other than those referred to in the chapter. I often encourage persons I am coaching to read certain resources that may be beneficial to their current situations, and they have always reported that they found them helpful. There are also appendixes in the back of the book that will assist the reader with sermon planning, computing pastoral compensation, and goal setting.

My Prayer for the Reader

I pray that you will be energized by the content of this book. One of the frustrations I felt in my twenty-year bivocational pastorate was the lack of resources that existed for ministers like me. Not many people seemed to understand God's call on my life, and even fewer appreciated it. I *do* understand your call to bivocational ministry, because that has been my call throughout my ministry, and I deeply appreciate what you bring to the kingdom of God.

I pray also that my ministry will add value to your ministry by providing resources that will inform and encourage you. This is my fourth book, and three of them have focused on bivocational ministry. In addition to the books, I maintain a website for bivocational ministers, www.bivocationalministries.com, to provide ongoing support for your ministry. I send out a free monthly e-newsletter to bivocational ministers, and you can be added to that mailing list by contacting me at dbickers@road-runner.com. I also serve as the project director for BivoNet, a ministry to the bivocational ministers in the American Baptist Churches USA.[2] As part of that work, I mail a quarterly newsletter to the bivocational ministers of that denomination. E-mail me at the above address to receive that newsletter. Finally, I am in the process of being certified as a Christian life coach,[3] and many of those I am currently coaching are bivocational ministers. You can find out more about coaching on my website, as well. I do all of this to offer you the resources and encouragement you need to fulfill God's call on your life, and I pray that you will find these useful.

PART ONE

The Work of the
Bivocational Minister

CHAPTER 1

What Is Bivocational Ministry?

Many people struggle to define bivocational ministry. Most would agree that a minister is bivocational if he or she has a job outside the church. But then other questions begin to come into play. Does it matter if the person works part-time or full-time in his or her other job? What about the minister who has retirement income from previous ministries or employment? Or how about the pastor of the large First Church who has book royalties or earns money through seminars and conferences? Would a student minister be considered bivocational?

Some questions deal more with the ministry provided by the minister than with his or her other employment. How many hours a week does a minister have to work in ministry to be considered full-time? If a person isn't full-time, is she or he a minister or simply a layperson providing ministry to the church in the absence of a regular pastor? How does ordination factor into the bivocational question?

A Simple Definition

I choose to define a bivocational minister as *anyone who serves in a paid ministry capacity in a church and has other personal sources of income.* This definition is not concerned with whether the person works full-time or part-time at the other job or with the sources of that other income. It does exclude ministers whose families are actually supported by the income generated by their spouses. Many small churches are able to keep a "full-time" pastor only because the spouse earns enough income to support the family, and this minister should not be considered bivocational, as he or she is not earning the additional income.

Throughout this book the reader will encounter a new term that many believe better reflects the work of the bivocational minister. In the past we have often heard ministers referred to as full-time or part-time. The problem with that is that ministry is never part-time work. As a bivocational pastor, I had the same number of sermons to prepare each year as the pastors of much larger churches. (In fact, I may have had more sermons to prepare because I didn't have people on staff to preach for me.) My members went into the hospital and expected pastoral visits. Church members and others in the community called upon me to conduct their weddings and officiate at their funerals. Like many pastors, I was on call 24/7, and I was excited to be involved in the lives of our congregation.

Rather than referring to full-time or part-time ministers, it is much better to call ministers either fully funded or bivocational. A fully funded minister is one who has no income other than that provided by the church, while the bivocational minister is one who does have other sources of personal income.

Opposition to Bivocational Ministry

Not everyone appreciates the new terminology. One fully funded pastor took great offense at my use of the term *fully funded*. He feels that he and many other ministers he knows are not adequately compensated by their churches for the work they do. Therefore, he was offended that anyone would refer to them as fully funded, but ironically he was not bothered by the implications of calling bivocational ministers "part-time."

Of course, not everyone appreciates bivocational ministry either. It is still seen by some people as a lesser ministry performed by persons who lack the skills or education needed to pastor a larger church. Although many who serve in this ministry do not hold a seminary degree, we will see in a later chapter that bivocational ministers often have more education than some people realize. Because many denominations require a master of divinity as the standard for ordination, however, that sends a message to bivocational ministers that they are second-class citizens in their denominations.

Many clergy see bivocational churches as undesirable and insignificant places to serve. In 1982 I was in a Christian bookstore and overheard a conversation by two recent seminary graduates, one of whom was a store employee. Asked if he had found a church to serve, he responded that the only churches that had called him were little churches out in the country, and he wasn't wasting his time with those churches. By that point in my ministry, I had been the pastor of Hebron, a small rural church, for about a year and certainly did not feel I was wasting *my* time. I was not sure what that young man considered ministry to be or what he had been taught at his seminary, but I was greatly offended by his attitude and left the store.

There is a growing appreciation for bivocational ministry across denominational lines, as well as in the emergent and missional church movements (see chapter 4). Unfortunately, some judicatories continue to neglect their bivocational churches, especially if they have been in decline for several years, have been inactive in the judicatory, and have contributed little financially to the judicatory. To a degree, given the financial difficulties experienced by many denominations today, this may be understandable, but it offers little chance for a struggling bivocational church to recover and once again provide an important ministry to its community. Such action by the judicatory also reinforces the message that these churches are no longer significant, which

4

adds to the poor self-image many bivocational churches have of themselves.

A number of people would prefer not to invest resources in bivocational churches. Instead, they would prefer either to close these churches or to merge two or more churches together to create one that would be large enough to support a fully funded minister. Such mergers seldom work well unless the churches are merged according to their strengths and each church is willing to vacate its own building and start the new merged church in another location. Few churches are interested in doing that unless there are significant problems with their existing facilities. In my opinion, a church that intentionally becomes bivocational and finds quality leadership has a much better likelihood of developing into a stronger, healthier church than a church that is a merger of two or more troubled churches.

Smaller, Not Lesser Ministry

The call to bivocational ministry is not a call to a lesser form of ministry, nor is it inferior in any way to the call to a fully funded ministry. It is simply a different call to meet different circumstances. Just as with fully funded ministers, bivocational ministers answer a call to provide important and needed leadership to a particular church or ministry.

And churches that call a bivocational minister should not feel that they are settling for second best. Many small churches have serious struggles with self-esteem issues.[1] Perhaps their membership has declined over the past several years and they fear God is finished with them. The fact that God calls a bivocational minister to serve them should be evidence enough that their ministry to the community is not finished. The church may find, like many bivocational churches before it, that new ministry opportunities lie ahead, and the future may be even more exciting than the past has been.

Key Characteristics of Bivocational Ministry

Bivocational ministry is similar to fully funded ministry in many aspects, but to be successful, it must have some key differences. We will look at some of those differences in this section, but for a deeper look at the many qualities that lead to a successful bivocational ministry, the reader may also refer to my earlier book *The Bivocational Pastor: Two Jobs, One Ministry*.[2]

Mutual Confidence in the Call

Perhaps the most crucial factor necessary for successful bivocational ministry is that both the church and the minister know they have been called to this ministry. Naturally, every pastor and congregation should experience a sense of divine calling to their shared ministry, but confidence in that calling is particularly critical for the bivocational minister and church.

A church that does not feel a definite call to be bivocational is more apt to develop a poor self-image based on a misplaced sense of inadequacy or inferiority. A church with such an image of itself will tend to project that image to others, including guests and prospective members. As a result, the poor self-image becomes a self-fulfilling prophecy because no one is attracted to a church that wonders if God has abandoned it.

Similarly, when a pastor serves as a bivocational minister but does not feel called to that ministry, she or he will often become angry and resentful—feeling like our friend in the bookstore that such ministry is "a waste of time." Such a minister is unlikely to be fully invested in the ministry and thus will experience few of its rewards.

The call to bivocational ministry is a definite call to a specific ministry for both the church and the minister, and how blessed both are when they respond to this call with joy and anticipation that God is going to do something powerful as a result! The church that understands that God is leading it to be bivocational

The Work of the Bivocational Minister

is excited that the Lord believes they have something important to offer the world and that they still have something to contribute to the kingdom of God. They can rejoice that God has provided pastoral leadership for them to continue their work.

Persons who know they have been called to bivocational ministry are happy to be involved in this form of ministry. One person recently sent me an e-mail in which he wrote, "As far as my greatest joys, the first is being able to share my faith with coworkers and customers who seldom if ever hear the gospel. Second, I find it a great joy to be free to listen to Jesus, obey him, and help others do the same without worrying about my paycheck." This individual does not see himself as a second-class minister, but as a person whom God is using in a great way to have a powerful impact in his community

Shared Ministry with the Laity

A second key characteristic of successful bivocational ministry is that laypersons are more involved in ministry. Some churches do better when they are without a pastor. When they have a pastor, they expect him or her to provide ministry to the church, but when the pastor leaves, people in the congregation step up to the plate and become more involved. As soon as they call a new pastor, they revert back to their bad habit of waiting for the pastor to do everything.

Bivocational churches seem to understand that their pastor does not have time to meet all the ministry needs in the church and community, and laypersons often assume many of those ministry responsibilities. This leads to a much healthier church that is more likely to grow.[3] Note that this characteristic requires the minister to be willing to ask people to become involved. Many people in the church are willing to help, but they seldom take the initiative. They may be afraid of offending the minister if they ask to take on some of his or her responsibilities. They may fear that they could not do the task as well as the minister,

which might hinder the work of the church. However, a bivocational minister has the powerful opportunity to invite the partic-
ipation of his or her members in the ministry of the church.
Generally, when members are asked to take on more responsibilities and are given the instruction and resources to do the job,
many are willing to respond—and the result is a congregation
that is growing in discipleship, leadership, and overall health.

Consent to a Simplified Structure
Many small churches are organized far beyond their needs. Some
of these report numerous committees and boards that would be
more suitable for a much larger congregation. In fact, their structures were usually developed when the church was much larger
and needed the various committees and boards to function. As
church attendance declined, the structure was never changed.
Even if they find people willing to serve, these committees and
boards seldom meet because they accomplish little and the people
are too busy to waste their time in unproductive meetings. Why
have committees that do not meet and boards that do not add
value to the church? Most likely, if the majority of committees in
most small churches never met again, there would be little or no
impact on the life of the church. A simple change in bylaws could
eradicate many of these groups, freeing up persons for activities
that would have a greater impact on the church and community.
    Bivocational churches are often more streamlined with fewer
committees, and meetings are often held on the same evening so
people don't have to attend meetings every night of the week. A
common reason for this is that the pastor simply does not have
time for meetings that add little value to the church. Many
Baptist churches have monthly deacon meetings, trustee meetings, and business meetings. When I was pastor at Hebron, we
had these meetings quarterly. Moreover, we combined the deacons and trustees and held their meeting an hour prior to the
business meeting. Our leaders only had to devote one night each

quarter to these meetings. If issues came up that needed immediate attention, a special meeting could always be arranged with a few phone calls. This allowed us to devote more time to ministry rather than keeping everyone busy with maintenance issues that make up the agenda of most meetings. Churches that share their minister's confidence in the bivocational calling and that invite shared ministry among the laity are also far more likely to agree to a simplified administrative and organizational structure. Such a simplified structure can accommodate the needs of the members as well as the demands on the time and energies of the bivocational minister.

Willingness to Work Hard

Lazy people will not last long in a bivocational setting. Adding the responsibilities of ministry to a forty-hour workweek will quickly become a burden to someone who doesn't enjoy work and doesn't believe that God has called her or him to both roles. I have observed that most bivocational ministers are type A personalities who are hardworking, aggressive, and competitive. Laziness is seldom a problem for these people. In fact, they may have to be careful that they do not become workaholics, and they will have to ensure that they intentionally maintain a healthy balance in their lives. We will explore maintaining balance further in chapter 5.

This willingness to work hard will often energize the members of a small church who may have been used to student pastors or retired ministers who primarily were at the church only on Sundays. As the members watch their pastor balance an outside job with ministry responsibilities, they may be challenged about their own level of commitment. The energy from their hardworking pastor may begin to transfer to them, leading them to become more actively involved in the life of the church and ministry to the community. Good things happen in the church when this occurs.

A Shepherding Ministry

Although the work of the minister has long been compared to that of a shepherd, in many churches today ministers function more like corporate CEOs. While the CEO model may work in megachurches, it is seldom successful in bivocational churches. Author and academic Doran McCarty is correct when he writes that the shepherd's role is a good image for the bivocational minister.[4]

Shepherds often work alone in a role considered undesirable by other people. Bivocational ministers are sometimes made to feel they are alone and not appreciated by their colleagues, especially their fully funded peers. They are seldom asked to speak at the annual meetings of their judicatories. Few are asked to write books or journal articles. However, they continue to serve their churches and care for the people entrusted to them by God. Every day they come home from their other jobs and prepare sermons, handle the administrative details, make hospital and nursing home visits, visit church members, and pray and seek God's direction for the future of their churches.

Shepherds identify with their sheep. Jesus once said that his sheep knew his voice, and the shepherds in the audience clearly understood the lesson. When sheep were intermingled with other flocks, the shepherd only had to call out or whistle and his or her sheep would come. Many bivocational ministers can identify more easily with their congregations because they often come from the same socioeconomic level, the same community, and the same theological understandings as the congregation. In larger churches a minister may struggle to know every member of the church by name, and in a megachurch such familiarity and intimacy is impossible. Bivocational ministers serving small churches not only can quickly learn the names of the church members, but can soon learn about their extended families and family history—sometimes more than they would prefer to know! This knowledge enables them to identify with their congregations and leads to greater trust between the minister and the congregation.

Shepherds care for their flock. They don't abandon the flock when wolves come looking for a meal; they protect the flock from predators. They seek out the wanderers and return them to the safety of the fold and make sure they have quiet waters from which to drink and good food to eat. Pastors, whether fully funded or bivocational, have a similar role and similar responsibilities in a congregation. They respond to Jesus' call to Peter: "Take care of my sheep" (John 21:16).

As we will discuss further in later chapters, bivocational ministers are found in both very small churches (as the only pastor) and in very large churches (as one of many associate ministers). In both extremes, congregations often experience high turnover in their leadership. The church I served had an average pastoral tenure of about one year before I became the pastor. I stayed twenty years. That doesn't mean there weren't times when I wanted to leave. Difficult times cause every minister to think about dusting off the résumé, and I was no exception. But when a shepherd knows and loves the people God entrusts to his or her care, as we have established many bivocational ministers have the privilege to do, that shepherd is more likely to stay and work through the issues.

Shepherds follow the sheep. McCarty notes that while in Jerusalem one morning, he noticed a shepherd sitting on a rock watching his flock. Later in the day he found that the shepherd was still sitting on that same rock waiting for the flock to move. When the sheep were ready to move, the shepherd would move with them.

Trying to drive a church in a direction they are not ready to go will result in failure and will probably lead to a short pastorate. This may be even more true in a bivocational congregation with highly involved laity and a simplified organizational structure. These churches need leaders, but if the minister gets too far ahead of the church, the members are likely to think the leader is the enemy and start shooting! Patience is especially crucial in leading a bivocational church, and the wise minister will not try to move the congregation until it is ready to move.

One bivocational pastor learned this lesson the hard way. He had served his church for two years and had seen attendance nearly double. He felt that the church needed to make several changes and proceeded to make them without consulting anyone. Longtime leaders in the church did not approve of the changes and were upset that they were not given an opportunity to discuss the changes before the pastor implemented the new strategies in the church. As the conflict began to intensify, the pastor called me for advice. He tried to repair the damage he had caused but would not compromise on the changes he wanted to make. A few weeks later he was asked to resign. This was a conflict that might have been prevented if the pastor had led the church and not tried to push it in a direction it wasn't ready to go.

Bivocational churches need pastoral leadership if they are to move forward, but they must be allowed to move at a pace with which they are comfortable. Changes can be presented to the church by the pastor, but the church must have time to think through what those changes will mean for them. Lay leaders and members have to be given permission to decide if they are ready to make those changes or not. Perhaps the best advice I can give bivocational leaders is to lead slowly.

Recommended Resources

Blackaby, Henry, and Richard Blackaby. *Spiritual Leadership: Moving People on to God's Agenda*. Nashville: Broadman & Holman, 2001.

Daman, Glenn. *Shepherding the Small Church: A Leadership Guide for the Majority of Today's Churches*. Grand Rapids: Kregel, 2002.

Dorr, Luther M. *The Bivocational Pastor*. Nashville: Broadman, 1988.

Dudley, Carl S. *Effective Small Churches in the Twenty-first Century*. Revised edition. Nashville: Abingdon, 2003.

Hansen, David. *The Power of Loving Your Church: Leading through Acceptance and Grace*. The Pastor's Soul Series. Edited by David L. Goetz. Minneapolis: Bethany House, 1998.

Kotter, John P. *Leading Change*. Boston: Harvard Business School Press, 1996.

London, H. B., Jr., and Neil B. Wiseman. *The Heart of a Great Pastor: How to Grow Strong and Thrive Wherever God Has Planted You*. Ventura, CA: Regal Books, 1994.

Pappas, Anthony G., ed. *Inside the Small Church*. Bethesda, MD: Alban Institute, 2002.

CHAPTER 2

Why Choose Bivocational Ministry?

Some believe that bivocational ministry is something new, but it is actually the way most ministers served until fairly recently. We not only see examples of bivocational ministry in the New Testament, but a study of church history will show that many ministers supported themselves and their families with employment outside the church.

New Testament Examples

The clearest example in the New Testament of a bivocational minister is the apostle Paul, who supported himself as a tentmaker (Acts 18:2-3). This would have been in accordance with the practice of rabbis in Paul's time who believed that every rabbi must practice some trade to support himself. William Barclay writes that this "meant that they never became detached scholars and always knew what the life of the working-man was like."[1] Because Aquila and Priscilla were also tentmakers, Paul stayed with them while he was in Corinth, where they shared not only a trade but also a ministry.

This does not mean that Paul did not accept support for his ministry from the churches. One of his arguments in 2 Corinthians 11 is that he had preached the gospel in Corinth free of charge because other churches supported his ministry. In Acts 18:5 Paul mentions that Silas and Timothy came to him from Macedonia while he was in Corinth. In 2 Corinthians 11:9 he says that what he lacked was supplied by the brethren who came to him from Macedonia. It seems clear that Silas and Timothy were given money from the churches in Macedonia, particularly the church in Philippi (Philippians 4:10-15), to support Paul's ministry. Thus, Paul's ministry was partially supported by the church and partially by his work as a tentmaker.

Historical Examples

Luther Dorr, a former professor at New Orleans Theological Seminary, writes that "Baptists and Methodists in particular owe a deep debt of gratitude to the farmer/preacher and the school teacher/preacher of the seventeenth and eighteenth centuries. These men followed the people to the frontier and supported themselves in order to preach the gospel."[2] In addition to the Baptists and Methodists, most Presbyterian ministers serving on the American frontier farmed, taught school, and held other jobs to supplement their church income.[3] Many of these churches made no effort to support their pastors, because they believed that paid clergy was too much like the state-subsidized ministries of the established churches. Doran McCarty believes that bivocational ministry was the norm among Southern Baptists until churches were encouraged by the denomination to seek full-time pastoral leadership around 1940.[4]

Current Bivocational Settings

Some people act as if bivocational ministry is a new phenomenon, but it has always continued to exist in small rural and urban churches. What did happen, however, is that many denominations virtually wrote off those churches that did not make the change to fully funded leadership and began to question the calling of persons who continued to serve as bivocational ministers. Although one can still find resistance to bivocational ministry, a number of Protestant denominations now recognize that their churches are becoming increasingly dependent on this form of leadership, and they are also recognizing the quality of ministry that often exists in a bivocational setting.

One will most likely continue to find bivocational ministry in small rural and urban communities. Many of these churches may have been filled with people and exciting ministries at one time but for one reason or another have seen their membership steadily decline over the years. As one who visits numerous small churches each year, I continue to be amazed at how many of them will have mounted on a wall an old black-and-white photo of the people who attended a church homecoming or some other special event in the life of the church. There are usually so many people in the picture that one can only wonder how they all fit in that small church building, and one also wonders where they all went.

The church I served for many years, Hebron Baptist Church, was a rural church that once filled its sanctuary every week. One member in the church remembers a time when they would open the windows during the summer and people would sit outside the church building on blankets to listen to the sermon because there wasn't enough room for everyone to come inside.

In 1940 an event occurred that changed the life of that church forever. The U.S. Army bought 56,000 acres about one mile from the church to use as a munitions testing facility. People, including many members of the church, were forced to sell their farms and move away. A fence was constructed around the land, cutting off all roads from one side of the county to the other, which prevented some members from easily being able to drive to the church. Attendance plummeted and never recovered. The church went from having a strong, viable ministry in the community to having one that struggled to survive. Similar stories can be told about other churches across this nation. The good news about this church is that it did survive and was able to find a new ministry with bivocational leadership.

Today's Growing Need for Bivocational Ministry

The need for bivocational ministers today is great and will continue to grow. One factor driving this is finances. The Pulpit and Pew Project of Duke Divinity School surveyed 883 clergy in 2001 to determine salary ranges among various size churches and different denominations. They classified the Protestant churches in two categories: connectional congregations, such as Methodists, Lutherans, and Presbyterians, which had some centralized guidelines regarding clergy salaries; and congregational churches, such as Baptists, Pentecostals, and the United Church of Christ, which had more freedom to determine their clergy compensation.

The median salary for connectional churches averaging one hundred or fewer attendees each week was $36,000, and the median salary for the congregational churches that size was $22,300. Moving to the next size church, 101–350 in attendance, the connectional churches had a median salary of $49,835, and the congregational churches had a median salary of $41,051.[5]

Of course, salaries are not the only financial consideration. Medical insurance continues to climb each year, putting a huge burden on the small church. Medical insurance costs for the minister's family can easily top $1,000 a month. One pastor of a church that averaged about seventy-five people each Sunday morning did not receive a salary increase for three years because it was all the church could do to continue to pay the insurance benefits for the pastor and his family.

Adding other benefits to the pastor's financial package, such as Social Security offset, mileage, retirement benefits, continuing education costs, convention costs, and a book allowance, is almost unheard of in small churches. However, these are benefits that ministers are entitled to receive, and at some stage of the minister's life, he or she will begin to look for a church that will provide those benefits.

Small churches are often the first churches that new seminary graduates serve, and these graduates often begin their ministries facing the prospects of repaying student loans, starting a family, and maintaining a home. These things are difficult to do with the salaries indicated in the above study. We should not be surprised then that within two or three years they feel the need to move to another church; nor should we condemn them for that. Ministers have an obligation to support their families.

This is one reason why small churches often suffer from frequent pastoral changes. Every two or three years the pastor resigns and the church begins a search for a new minister. This search may take a few months or it may take a year or longer. The church spends most of its time seeking a pastor and getting to know that new leader before he or she leaves and the process starts over. Without a longer pastorate, the church is unlikely to experience any significant growth and break this cycle. But a longer pastorate is unlikely unless the church can call a bivocational minister who will not be completely dependent on the church for his or her income.

Small Churches Are Bigger

Being able to adequately pay a pastor is not just a problem for a church of fifty or sixty people. It is a problem faced by many churches twice that size. In his excellent book *Small Congregation, Big Potential*, Lyle Schaller defines a small church as one that averages 125 or fewer in worship.[6] In another book he predicted that many churches this size might soon be led by teams of bivocational ministers.[7] This means that bivocational ministers might soon be serving in larger churches than normally associated with this type of ministry.

Bivocational ministers serving in larger churches will represent a major paradigm shift for many denominations, churches, and ministers. A church of 125 people is considered a rather healthy church in many traditions. If Schaller's predictions are true, these traditions will have to reexamine how they assign or recommend ministers to these churches. The churches will wonder why they suddenly struggle to support a fully funded minister when nothing has changed in their attendance patterns. Ministers often move to this size church after their first pastorate, but it may no longer be worthwhile for them to do so if they are unable to meet the growing financial needs of their families.

Fewer Ministers Are Willing to Serve Small Churches

In the introduction I referred to a study by Patricia Chang that found that few ministers were willing to serve small churches. While finances may play a role in their decisions, other factors come into play as well. Some ministers are not comfortable living in a rural or urban setting where many small churches are located. They may fear their spouses will have difficulty finding employment in their chosen fields in a small community. Some want to continue their education and therefore seek to live near seminaries and universities. They may want the conveniences of living in or near a larger city. They may believe their children would have more opportunities and enjoy better schools in a larger community. Some believe a suburban area is a safer place in which to raise a family.

Some of these ministers also see the small church as an undesirable place to serve. Small churches are often plateaued and resistant to change. Many do not show much potential for growth. The facilities are often dated and sometimes in poor repair. Many lack video projection equipment, a good sound system, and other equipment seen as essential to ministry in the twenty-first century. The recent seminary graduate who is more comfortable with Greek and Hebrew than with relationships might feel that she or he would not be a good fit in these churches and would probably be right.

The Shrinking Middle

Another factor that will lead to an increased need for bivocational ministers is that medium-sized churches are either growing much larger or are shrinking to small church size. Lyle Schaller reports that while a few churches that averaged seventy-five to eighty in the 1980s have grown, a much larger number of them have shrunk in size and become small churches.[8] Many of these churches will resist becoming bivocational, but it may be the only way they can survive and find a new purpose and ministry.

Specialized Ministries

Like it or not, Christians and non-Christians alike often come to our churches with a consumer mind-set. They expect the church to offer the programs they need, and they expect excellence in those programs. Pastors used to be generalists, but the demand for more excellent programming requires greater abilities than many pastors possess. Few pastors are dynamic speakers, compassionate care shepherds, energetic youth group leaders, accomplished choir directors, and competent administrators all rolled into one. Pastors therefore need persons skilled in some of these areas to come alongside them and provide leadership in the areas where they are lacking.

Many churches cannot afford to add fully funded staff, but if expectations of excellence are not met, people may leave and go to churches that can meet their expectations. One does not have to agree that this is the way things should be in the church, but if it is the reality, the church must decide how it will address it. The two primary ways of addressing this challenge are to ignore it and let people leave or to find persons to join the church staff and lead these specialized ministries. In many cases churches are finding that they are able to add bivocational people to these roles.

New Church Planting

A number of evangelical and mainline churches have discovered that the best way to reach new people with the gospel of Jesus Christ is to start new churches. Some are started in communities that have no other church of that denomination, some target specific groups of people whose needs are not currently being met, and others focus on certain minority groups that may be moving into the area. Many of these new church plants are being led by bivocational ministers.

New church planting is expensive, and some denominations have set some challenging goals for the number of new churches they want to start. Using bivocational church planters can save these denominations a lot of money that can be used to start other churches.

Ed Stetzer correctly points out that God, not a denomination, calls someone to start a church, and lack of finances should never be used as an excuse not to plant a church. He encourages church planters who do not have sufficient finances to start as bivocational church planters at least until the church grows enough to support the pastor.[9] Stetzer and other church planter authorities agree that even if the church planter has sufficient funds to start a church, she or he should work outside the church until attendance reaches two hundred. This puts the church planter into the community and provides contact with people who can be invited to become part of the new church. It will also set the standard that the church planter will not always be available and the church will have to resolve some issues on their own.[10]

Growth of Missional Churches

According to Ron Carlson, missional church strategist for National Ministries of the American Baptist Churches USA, "A missional church is a community of faith that directs its ministry focus primarily outward toward the context in which it is located and toward the broader world beyond. Missional churches recognize that they exist in a post-denominational, post-Christendom world in which it is imperative for churches to 'go into the world' of the unchurched."

Many churches are becoming more missional in the way they approach ministry. They recognize that mission is not something that is merely done by someone else in some other part of the world. The mission field exists just outside the door of the church and throughout the community. To impact that mission field, however, the church will have to learn the culture and the language of the mission field. Every member of the church will have to become a missionary, and missionaries are often tentmakers.

We will likely see an increase in ministers becoming bivocational by choice to better relate to the mission field the church wants to reach. This may be especially true in churches that make an intentional choice to remain small and plant new churches throughout their communities to have a more effective impact.

Revolutionaries

George Barna tells us that more than twenty million Americans now fit in a category he calls revolutionaries.[11] These are Christians who believe that the established church is hazardous to their spiritual health. Not satisfied with merely *going* to church, they want to *be* the church. Each week they gather in one another's homes to worship, and each week they go into the world to minister. Although not used in the traditional sense that we are using the word *bivocational* in this book, Barna would argue that all revolutionaries are bivocational. He writes, "Tent-making—the practice of working at a non-religious job as a means of paying the bills while facilitating one's desire to be a genuine representative of Christ in the world—moves from a quirky, first-century idea to a defining, personal lifestyle."[12]

If this movement continues to grow, some will rise to leadership status and receive a salary for their leadership. Due to the small size of these groups, such leaders will have to be bivocational to support themselves and their families.

Why Choose Bivocational Ministry?

Why should someone choose to become bivocational? For one, doing so means standing on some very broad shoulders—not the least of which are the apostle Paul's. We have already seen the substantial biblical and historical precedents for such ministry. A good argument could be made that bivocational ministry has a much longer track record than fully funded ministry. It is a valid call of God on a person's life to meet a specific need in a specific place. It is not superior to fully funded ministry, nor is it inferior. It is simply another form of ministry that God is using to impact the world.

A second reason to choose bivocational ministry is that the need for it is so great. Many churches can no longer afford to provide a living salary and benefit package for a fully funded minister. Does this mean the ministry of these churches is over? Perhaps in some cases; but the vast majority of these congregations can still provide much needed ministries to their communities if they can find someone to lead them. In most cases it will take a longer pastorate than two or three years to establish the trust that is needed and to discern God's vision for the future ministry of the church. Fully funded pastors are unlikely to stay at these churches long enough to do either. The hope of these churches and the potential impact these churches can have on their communities lie in finding a bivocational leader who will remain with them and provide the leadership the members need.

Along with the existing small churches that need bivocational leadership, the face of American churches is changing rapidly. Bivocational ministers can also be added to church staffs to provide specialized ministries the church needs but could not afford if they had to hire fully funded staff. New church plants and house churches are starting everywhere. In many cases, bivocational leadership makes sense for these churches.

The need for bivocational ministers is great and growing, but this is only part of the reason why someone should consider becoming a bivocational minister. The other half of that equation, and the most important reason, is that God is calling that person to do so. During my twenty years as pastor of Hebron Baptist Church, I had no doubt that God had called me to be the bivocational pastor of that church. I had numerous opportunities to go to other churches, but I was convinced that I was doing what God had called me to do.

Knowing that bivocational ministry is biblical, that it has historic precedent, and that the need for such ministers is great and growing is important. But knowing that you have been called by God to this type of ministry is the primary reason for choosing it. You may have sensed that God is calling you to bivocational ministry, but you just can't believe the Lord would call someone like you. You may doubt you have the gifts or abilities to serve in that way. In the next chapter we will take a look at people who currently serve in bivocational ministries. You may find they are a lot like you.

Recommended Resources

Bierly, Steve R. *How to Thrive as a Small-Church Pastor: A Guide to Spiritual and Emotional Well-Being.* Grand Rapids: Zondervan, 1998.

Clapp, Steve, Ron Finney, and Angela Zimmerman. *Preaching, Planning, and Plumbing: The Implications of Bivocational Ministry for the Church and for You—Discovering God's Call to*

Service and Joy. Fort Wayne, IN: Christian Community, 1999.

Elliott, John Y. *Our Pastor Has an Outside Job: New Strength for the Church Through Dual Role Ministry*. Valley Forge, PA: Judson Press, 1980.

Klassen, Ron, and John Koessler. *No Little Places: The Untapped Potential of the Small-Town Church*. Grand Rapids: Baker, 1996.

Lowery, James L., Jr. *Bi-Vocationals: Men and Women Who Enrich the Human Ecology and the World Surrounding*. West Conshohocken, PA: Infinity, 2006.

PART TWO

Bivocational Ministry in Context

CHAPTER 3

Who Is the Bivocational Minister?

There is no "typical" bivocational minister. We are a diverse group of people who have had a wide variety of life experiences that we bring into our ministries.

In January 2004 I sent surveys to 612 persons who had been identified as bivocational ministers in the American Baptist Churches USA by their regional offices. The information gleaned from the 110 who responded will be used throughout this chapter to help us better understand the individuals who provide leadership to bivocational churches. When possible we will also compare the findings of my survey with other studies that have been done on bivocational ministers.

Personal Information

According to most surveys, the majority of bivocational ministers are men over the age of fifty, serving as the senior (or sole) pastor of their church. The vast majority have served their congregations for less than ten years; the average tenure of a bivocational pastorate is just shy of six years, with male pastors averaging slightly longer and females slightly shorter tenures. Only 6 percent of respondents had served the same church for twenty years or more. Thirty-three percent of the bivocational respondents were serving in their first church.

The average age of the bivocational ministers was 53.5. Because many individuals enter bivocational ministry later in life or
after retirement, the average age should not be surprising. I
recently spoke to two men who may take early retirement from
their employers in eleven years. Both of them will be in their early
fifties when they retire. They wanted to know if now would be
a good time to start taking classes so they can become pastors
after retiring. One has since informed me that he is now enrolled
in seminary and pursuing his master's degree.

The majority of the responders to my modest survey were Euro-
American, but those numbers would be dramatically different
with a broader sampling. Pastor and consultant Dr. Lincoln
Bingham recently reported that about two-thirds of the African
American pastors in Kentucky are bivocational.[1] Bivocational
ministers are found in every racial category.

Author and researcher Deborah Bruce of Research Services for
the Presbyterian Church (USA) in Louisville, Kentucky, conducted
a survey of bivocational ministers in that denomination and had
very similar findings. She received 109 returned surveys and
found that the majority were male (86 percent) and that 60 percent were over the age of 50. The largest group of responders to
her survey was senior pastors (46 percent). One-fourth of the
people in her survey had been in bivocational ministry less than
five years. Sixty percent had served in previous bivocational ministries prior to the church they were currently serving.[2]

Education

Some people believe that bivocational ministry is primarily for
persons who can serve only in small congregations because they
lack formal education and theological training, but my survey did
not find that to be the case. Just 24.5 percent who responded to
the survey had completed their education with only a high school
diploma. Thirty-seven percent had attended college, and 42 percent were seminary graduates. Twenty percent of them have a

master of divinity, and 14.5 percent have other master's degrees. Six percent have a doctor of ministry, and another 5 percent have earned other doctorates.

A study conducted by Dr. L. Ronald Brushwyler and the Midwest Ministry Development Service in 1992 found even higher educational levels among the 106 midwestern bivocational pastors they interviewed. They found that "ninety-six percent were college graduates, 33 percent had master's degrees other than seminary, 96 percent were seminary graduates, and 20 percent had doctorates."[3] Whatever reasons these ministers may have had for being bivocational, a lack of education was not one of them.

I am acquainted with a minister who has a PhD from Princeton University who served as the bivocational pastor of a small rural church for a number of years while also serving as the director of a counseling center and as an associate professor of a seminary. I know of another bivocational pastor who has served a small, rural church for many years who is also the vice president of a university. Either of these ministers could serve fully funded churches, but they feel called to the work they are doing and to serving as pastors to small churches.

Not all bivocational ministers began their ministries with college and seminary degrees. Like me, they began their education *after* becoming bivocational ministers. I had been the pastor of Hebron for a little over a year when I decided that I needed further education if I wanted to grow as a minister. I enrolled in a two-year Bible college, and after graduating from that program, I began studies at a local college to earn a bachelor's degree. Due to my work and ministry, it took me seven years to earn that degree. Earlier this year I graduated from seminary with my master's degree. I have since been accepted into a doctor of ministry program and will soon begin my first course. Although working a full-time job, pastoring a church, caring for a family, and attending college and seminary is not easy, it is doable, and many bivocational ministers have taken that route to further their education and to improve their ministry gifts.

The fact that many bivocational ministers do not have seminary degrees can present a problem for those denominations that consider the master of divinity a requirement for ordination recognition. If denominations are going to be serious about recognizing the importance of bivocational ministry, they will need to address the educational requirements for ordination. (Some are already developing seminary "equivalency" programs.) It may be that an educational standard for ordination is an outdated requirement better suited for ministry in an earlier time and not for the postmodern period in which we now minister.

Continuing Education

Although bivocational ministers tend to be well educated, many are not involved in continuing education. It was very disturbing to learn that almost half of those responding to my study had not attended any continuing education event related to ministry in the previous three years. Another 23 percent had attended two or fewer events.

These same individuals *do* attend continuing education events for their other employment. One bivocational pastor also teaches school. He reported that in the past three years he had attended fifty-four continuing education events as a teacher and none as a pastor.

Persons in the medical, legal, educational, and accounting fields are required to have a certain amount of continuing education on a regular basis to maintain their credentials. Even the service technicians who work in my heating and air-conditioning company are required to have a minimum of ten hours of documented training each year to keep their licenses. Yet in a time of rapid changes in our society and in the church, persons who have responsibility for the well-being of eternal souls spend little or no time in continuing education.

This is certainly not due to a lack of opportunities. Many denominations, seminaries, middle judicatories, parachurch organizations, churches, and individuals offer a wide variety of continuing education events every year. Seldom does a week go by that ministers do not receive numerous invitations to attend some event that could be beneficial to their ministry.

Ministers gave two primary reasons for not attending such events. The major reason was time constraints. Many continuing education events for ministers are held while bivocational ministers are working at their other jobs. It is very difficult for them to attend such events unless they use vacation time, and then they feel they are depriving their families of much needed time together. It should not be surprising that the overwhelming majority of respondents to my survey said that Saturdays are the best time for them to attend continuing education events. But even when such events are held on Saturdays, many bivocational ministers still will not attend, because that is also the best day for them to do a number of things either related to ministry, family activities, or self-care.

The second reason the ministers gave for not attending continuing education events is that they have found previous events of little benefit to their ministries. Although this seems to be changing some, most continuing education events have been primarily for larger churches than most bivocational ministers serve.

In the twenty-first century, denominations and judicatories will need to take a close look at the training events they offer and when they are offered. First, denominations will need to understand that getting bivocational ministers to attend continuing education events is difficult, even when the events are developed for them, with their unique programming and planning needs in mind. Until the word gets out that these events are being developed primarily for them and that the events are being done with excellence, many bivocational ministers will continue to avoid continuing education events as one commitment they do not have time to make.

Other Occupations

Bivocational ministers can be found working almost any other job one can imagine. A few years ago, one bivocational minister reported on a Web chat site that he was a card dealer in Nevada. (Others on the site responded that they weren't sure if that was a suitable occupation for a minister, and we never heard from him again.) Persons responding to my survey didn't report any occupation quite so interesting. A large number work as educators, including several who teach at the college and seminary level. Many reported that they work in sales and management. Others identified various forms of ministry as their second occupation, for example, counseling, chaplaincy, and social work. A few serve as policemen or correctional officers. A number are self-employed, such as farmers and entrepreneurs operating their own businesses.

Denominational Connection

Brushwyler found a great desire of bivocational ministers to be connected to their denominations,[4] but I found in my study that many bivocational ministers are unaware of the denominational resources available to them or uninvested in their denomination's efforts. For example, only about one-third of the responders belong to our denomination's Ministers Council, and even fewer are registered in the denomination's personnel profile system. A few reported that they did not even know that these things existed. Based on the answers given to other questions, it was also apparent that several were not familiar with denominational terminology. None of the bivocational congregations represented in the study gave large sums of money to denominational mission work. In fact, the churches gave almost as much to mission efforts *not* sponsored by their denomination as they gave to the denomination's mission work.

Salary and Benefits

As might be expected, most bivocational ministers are not paid very well for their ministry work. (Most fully funded ministers can say the same!) In my survey, the highest annual salary reported by a bivocational male pastor was $26,430, and the highest reported salary for a female pastor was $24,000. The average salary for male ministers was $9,770, and for female ministers it was $8,578. What makes those averages more significant is that many pastors receive no additional benefits from their church or denomination. We will consider those options more extensively in chapter 5.

It comes as a surprise to some bivocational churches that they are legally required to provide their pastor with a W-2 form (not merely a 1099) and to report her or his income to the Internal Revenue Service. A few churches do not provide their pastors with any form and do not report the income the pastor receives to the IRS. These churches and ministers can incur severe penalties if they are ever audited. The minister is also being deprived of future Social Security benefits on the income not being reported. Properly reporting the minister's salary and providing W-2 forms are not difficult, but if the church treasurer does not feel comfortable doing this, he or she should seek assistance from a tax advisor or CPA. The cost of being in compliance is much less than possible future penalties.

Ministry Satisfaction

It seems obvious that bivocational ministers do not serve for the financial benefits, so what *does* lead a person to consider this type of ministry? Sixty-eight percent of the bivocational ministers Brushwyler studied reported that they were bivocational by choice and felt committed to this form of ministry.[5] Bruce reported similar findings from her study.[6]

Some bivocational ministers have previously served as fully funded pastors. In some cases the church experienced financial difficulties and could no longer afford to pay a fully funded pastor, and the minister chose to become bivocational rather than going to another church. Some returned to fully funded ministry at a later time, but others realized they preferred bivocational ministry and felt specifically called to it. Of course, not everyone currently serving as a bivocational minister appreciates the role. However, those who feel *called* to this form of ministry report very high satisfaction rates.

Could You Do Bivocational Ministry?

We see from this chapter that there really is no such thing as a "typical" bivocational minister. Such a person may be male or female and come from a wide variety of educational and occupational backgrounds. God calls bivocational ministers from every race and age level. The only thing that really matters is having that call on one's life. If God is calling you to bivocational ministry, then God will make a way past the barriers—and you will discover Paul's joy in being content in every situation.

Recommend Resources

Bickers, Dennis W. *The Tentmaking Pastor: The Joy of Bivocational Ministry*. Grand Rapids: Baker, 2000.

Dorr, Luther M. *The Bivocational Pastor*. Nashville: Broadman, 1988.

Lowery, James L., Jr. *Bivocationals: Men and Women Who Enrich the Human Ecology and the World Surrounding*. West Conshohocken, PA: Infinity, 2006.

CHAPTER 4

Where Can You Find Bivocational Ministry?

Bivocational ministry is found in many different settings, but the most common setting is the small church. At one time some of these churches may have been larger churches with fully funded pastors, but for a variety of reasons they have lost membership and have decided they would have to become bivocational or cease to exist. It was in such a church that I began my pastoral ministry.

As mentioned in an earlier chapter, Hebron Baptist Church was once a very healthy, strong rural church until the U.S. Army purchased much of the land where the church members lived. The congregation declined rapidly at that point and, for a number of years, was served by student pastors from a seminary about an hour away.

Small Church Settings

Hebron's experience is very similar to that of many rural churches in our area. One should not assume that because a church is small it is unhealthy or that it is not interested in reaching new people. There are many reasons beyond the control of churches that can cause them to become and remain small. Obviously, most people in the church did not want to sell their farms to the U.S. Army and move away, but no one could prevent that from happening. A church cannot stop a major employer from closing its factory and moving its manufacturing overseas, but the churches in a community where that happens will be affected by that decision. Churches cannot stop natural disasters such as hurricanes from occurring, but they can be greatly impacted if people are unable to rebuild and therefore move to other parts of the country.

As an area resource minister for my denomination, I serve seventy-eight churches in my area. Half of these churches average fifty or fewer people on Sunday mornings. Many of them were led for years by students from the same seminary that provided pastors for Hebron. Even though this seminary was of a different denomination than these churches, the churches automatically contacted the seminary's placement office when they needed a new pastor. For a number of reasons, our churches have found it much more difficult to obtain students from this seminary to serve as their pastors. These churches are now looking for bivocational leadership, and in many cases they are finding that their bivocational ministers are providing much better leadership than they received from the students.

Many small churches see themselves as training centers for pastors pursuing their theological degrees. The student pastors often see their small church pastorate as a way to receive some experience, satisfy their field education requirements, and receive some money to help support them while they attend seminary. Few go to these small churches expecting to stay there beyond their seminary graduation. Most are usually on the field only on weekends unless there is an emergency at the church. While both the churches and the student pastors may benefit from their relationships, this does not seem to be an appropriate way to view ministry.

These small churches are part of the body of Christ and have a God-ordained purpose, and I do not believe that purpose is to be a training center for pastors to prepare them to move on to a "significant" ministry elsewhere. Every church is a significant ministry that God wants to use to impact the community in which it has been placed. It is unlikely that such ministry will be achieved in the eighteen months or so the student pastor is willing to commit to the church.

Bivocational pastors often remain at the church for longer periods of time (see chapter 6 for more information on pastoral tenures). This allows the church to establish a relationship with the pastor, leading to a deeper level of trust in his or her leadership. It also enables the pastor to better understand the church and the community and to develop a ministry that will better serve both. Hebron and I enjoyed a very good relationship during my pastorate, and we shared a significant ministry there that touched the lives of many people.

I mentioned in the introduction the church led by Pat Lanman. This church was served by student pastors for many years until they called Lanman as their bivocational minister. During their student pastorates, the church declined and finally plateaued at around thirty people. The church now averages nearly twice that many people and has an excellent ministry to young people in the county. Furthermore, the church has started a ministry in Appalachia that is touching the lives of people who live four hours away from the church. Even more exciting is that other small churches in the area are now participating in this Appalachia ministry, enabling them to serve even more people in that part of the country. This small church now has a significant ministry to its community and to a region of the country two hundred miles away. It has also been able to bring together other churches in its association to be involved in that ministry. None of this is likely to have happened without the capable leadership of their bivocational pastor.

I do not mean for this section to be critical of seminary students serving as pastors of small churches. An entire book could be written, and probably should be, on the pros and cons of such ministry. Here I can only say that in twenty-five years of working with small churches, I have never seen a church develop a strong ministry with student pastors who leave soon after graduation. I have, however, witnessed numerous small churches grow and experience exciting ministries under the leadership of bivocational ministers.

One of the keys to a successful bivocational ministry in the small church is that the minister and the congregation must agree on the minister's priorities. Bivocational ministry cannot work if the congregation is not willing to assume some ministry responsibilities. When we began to have several people visiting our church, I told our deacons that I could not visit our guests and regularly visit all our members. I suggested they tell me which group they wanted me to focus on, and they would become responsible for the other group. They asked me to concentrate on our guests and prospective members, and they would minister to the needs of our members. It was a good arrangement that ensured that both our church guests and members received ministry.

Some mind-sets may have to be changed for the sharing of responsibilities to work well. We often talk about pastoral care as if such ministry is wholly the work of the pastor, but for pastoral care to be done well, a ministry partnership must exist between the church and the pastor. In *The Pastor's Guide to Effective Ministry*, Ron Blake is correct when he writes, "Pastoral care no longer assumes the pastor is the sole caregiver. In today's culture, pastoral care involves and engages congregational care."[1]

Multistaff Church Settings

Recently I had lunch with a pastor who leads a church averaging 350 people on Sunday morning. For a number of years, the church had a fully funded associate pastor who was primarily responsible for the youth ministry in the church. The pastor told me that the church has now eliminated the fully funded position and added four bivocational persons to meet specific needs in the youth program. Their youth program is now more defined according to ages and needs. This church already has a strong youth ministry that involves nearly one hundred young people, and this move is expected to make this program even stronger.

Ministers have typically been seen as generalists. We have been expected to be all things to all people. In the twenty-first century, we will have to end this lone ranger mentality by implementing ministry teams.[2] Pollster George Barna writes, "In my research with churches across the nation, I have recognized two realities: First, quality leadership is indispensable to ministry success (defined as consistent and widespread life transformation), and second, we expect too much of individual leaders."[3] People's expectations and needs are too great for any one person to meet, and even small and medium-sized churches are going to need more specialists who can focus on specific needs in the church and community.

This may not be a problem for the largest churches, but it will become very difficult for other congregations to provide more focused ministry with fully funded staff. However, many churches can add bivocational people to their staffs, enabling programming that will attract more people. It will also allow staff members to focus their efforts primarily on their areas of giftedness.

I am currently assisting a church that is seeking a new pastor. The church wants a pastor who can lead them in growing in size by reaching out to the community. At the same time, the primary gifts the congregation says they want in their pastor are pastoral care and communication gifts. I suggested to the committee that it can be very difficult to find a pastor with these gifts who is also an excellent outreach minister. My recommendation to them was that they consider calling two ministers, one or both of whom would be bivocational. The pastor would be a person gifted in leading the church in outreach efforts, and the other minister would be someone who could provide pastoral care to the membership. This person could even be a retired pastor seeking to supplement his or her retirement income while providing an important ministry to the church.

My friend Leon Wilson pastored a church in Oklahoma that grew to more than six hundred people on Sunday mornings. He and his staff of six ministers were all bivocational by choice. You can read a little more about his ministry in chapter 6, but his is not the only large church that is intentionally led by bivocational ministers.

Bivocational staff will provide the church with some new challenges. Bringing all the staff together for planning meetings may be difficult due to the different work schedules involved. Taking the entire staff to a continuing education event may be impossible for the same reason. Work schedules sometimes change, preventing a staff member from participating in some events, including some for which he or she may have responsibility. For example, some factories now have mandatory overtime that requires workers to work evenings or weekends. I recommend some overlapping of responsibilities between bivocational staff so that one person does not have all the knowledge about any given event. Adding bivocational staff is an excellent way to add more focus to specific ministries in the church, but it also requires a great deal of flexibility and some rethinking about how staff will relate to one another and work together.

New Church Plants

Many Protestant denominations have learned that starting new churches is the best way to reach new people with the gospel. These denominations have made church planting a priority and have developed specific strategies for starting these new churches. Some strategies call for sending a team of specially trained ministers who are funded by the denomination into a community to start the new church. Other strategies use bivocational ministers who are expected to raise much of their own support through their other jobs. Both strategies have certain advantages and disadvantages.

The advantage of having a bivocational church planter is that it does not require as much money from the founding denomination. This allows the denomination to start more new churches with less money, and it provides the church planter with a sense of financial security. She or he does not have to worry about the denomination's funds drying up before the church plant becomes financially sound. It also places the planter in the workplace, providing more opportunities for contact. Although I never served as a church planter, an important part of my ministry was to the factory workers with whom I worked for thirty years. Ministering to coworkers and building relationships with them can help add persons to the new church plant.

A disadvantage of bivocational church planting is that it reduces the amount of time one can focus on ministry. Few things are more difficult than trying to build something from the ground up, and church planting is no exception. It is challenging and time-consuming. Having another job adds to the stress. Still, many church planters are bivocational, and they have been able to overcome the challenges and establish strong, healthy new churches.

Denominations aren't the only ones starting new churches. Many independent churches are committed to starting churches to reach people where they are. They encourage their members to seek opportunities to start churches, and some of them find creative new ways to do so.

One young man in his thirties came to church one night to announce that he had started a new church that meets at 3:00 A.M. in a supermarket parking lot. He worked as a security officer at night and found a number of people who also worked nights and slept during the day. They had been unable to attend church until this young man started one that could meet when they were able to attend.[4] He did not need denominational support, because his other job provided him with income.

Bivocational Ministry in Context

Community Ministry Context

A minister who graduated from Bible school with me served a church for a number of years as a fully funded pastor. After he resigned from that church, he became the director of a relief shelter in a large, nearby city. Recently he felt called back into pastoral ministry but did not want to leave the work he was doing at the shelter. He now serves as a bivocational pastor while continuing as the director of the relief shelter. Because he feels called to both forms of ministry, this is a great opportunity for him, and he is able to use his gifts ministering in two vastly different fields.

Many community ministries are finding it difficult to raise sufficient funds to pay for staffing and ministry. Cutbacks in both are not uncommon, which means the ministry is losing good people and the people they serve are finding fewer resources available to them. Again, bivocational ministry allows available funds to go further and enables the minister to use more of her or his gifts while serving in both roles.

Such ministry can also have a positive impact on the church being served. Many small churches are rather maintenance-minded in their thinking. Survival is their primary focus. Although most of them will say they want to grow, a quick look at their budget and programming will show that almost everything they do is for the good (and survival) of the church. Having a pastor who is also involved in community ministry can bring enlightenment concerning the needs surrounding the church. This awareness may spark new attitudes about ministry and lead the church to become involved in ministries outside their own congregational needs.

Theological Education Context

John Chowning serves as the vice president for church and external relations and as executive assistant to the president at Campbellsville University in Campbellsville, Kentucky. He teaches part-time in the university's political science division. He also serves as the bivocational pastor of Saloma Baptist Church in Taylor County, Kentucky. Al Hardy is the dean of academic support at the same university and serves as the pastor of Good Hope Baptist Church. The reader should not be surprised to learn that this university has a strong School of Theology and a Center for Bivocational Ministries.

In an earlier study I conducted of bivocational ministers in the American Baptist Churches USA nearly 3 percent of respondents reported their other occupation was in a seminary or Bible school setting either as an administrator or educator. If someone asked Chowning, Hardy, and the others in my study, they would all agree that they feel equally called to both forms of ministry and that they derive much satisfaction from both.

Many advantages come from being involved in both bivocational ministry and theological education. These ministers have an opportunity to put into practice the ministry theories that are often taught but never field tested by many seminary professors. Teaching about church growth is one thing; actually growing a church is another. One can teach the principles of healthy churches without ever leading a healthy church. Many people can teach how to structure a Sunday school department in a seminary classroom, but what happens to that structure when there are only thirty people in the entire Sunday school? Some of what is taught in seminary might change if the instructors tried to implement their theories as bivocational ministers. At the very least, some of the classes might become more practical and relate better to what ministers actually face in pastoral ministry.

Another advantage of being a bivocational minister and an educator is that the educator-minister has access to the best research available to theological educators. In my years of working with bivocational ministers, I have found that many do not know what kind of information is available to help them do ministry nor how to access such information. I am frequently distressed when I see their libraries; I wonder how they can effectively prepare sermons and know the best ministry practices available today. Typically, they have very few books, and these are often more devotional than theological. Seldom do I find many books that have been recently published. I confess that I can hardly stay out of bookstores, so I may be overly sensitive, but at times I wonder if some bivocational ministers even know where their closest bookstore is. The theological educator/bivocational minister will not have that problem.

Having an educator as a pastor also benefits the church being served. The church is likely to profit from the education and continuous learning that is required of theological educators. Of course, the pastor-educator will need to tailor a sermon intended for a lay audience rather differently than a lecture intended for seminarians—not only in the language used but also in the substance and purpose of the message. Learning to speak and teach in the language of one's audience is a great exercise in Paul's practice of aiming to be all things to all people (1 Corinthians 9:22). Assuming the educator is theologically sound, the church should grow both spiritually and numerically from Scripture-based teaching and preaching. The church will also have access to the best ministry practices available for ministering in today's culture.

Bivocational Ministers Are Found in Many Settings

When I began my ministry bivocational ministers primarily served as pastors of smaller churches. Today there are many options available to the person called to this ministry. Not only are smaller churches seeking bivocational ministers to serve as their pastors but medium and larger churches are looking for bivocational persons to serve in staff positions. This allows the minister to utilize his or her gifts better and enables the church to offer more specialized ministries to the congregation and community. As one considers the call to this form of ministry it is important to be open to a wide variety of ministry options. This dynamic makes for a very exciting time for persons entering bivocational ministry.

Recommended Resources

Schaller, Lyle E. *Innovations in Ministry: Models for the 21st Century*. Nashville: Abingdon, 1994.

———. *Small Congregation, Big Potential: Ministry in the Small Membership Church*. Nashville: Abingdon, 2003.

Stetzer, Ed. *Planting Missional Churches: Planting a Church That's Biblically Sound and Reaching People in Culture*. Nashville: Broadman & Holman, 2006.

PART THREE

Challenges and Opportunities of Bivocational Ministry

CHAPTER 5

What Makes Bivocational Ministry Risky?

Bivocational ministers and their churches face many challenges. Some of these are typical of ministry in general, but some are unique to the bivocational setting. In this chapter we will first address some of the challenges and difficulties faced by the minister, and then we will examine those experienced by the church. The list of challenges is long, and they must be overcome if the church and minister are to enjoy a successful and joyous ministry together.

Challenges for the Minister

Time Management

Time management is the number one problem among bivocational ministers according to respondents of my survey. People who attend the workshops and conferences I lead also identify this as their greatest challenge. Time management is really life management, and the bivocational minister must find ways to properly manage his or her life.

Because I have addressed time management at length in my two previous books on bivocational ministry,[1] I will not devote much space to the topic here. I will, however, add a couple of suggestions. An excellent tool that will help ministers better manage their lives is a written statement of purpose for their lives. I am in the process of being certified as a life coach, and several of the persons I am now coaching are bivocational ministers. One mentioned that he was struggling in his efforts to devote sufficient time to all the things that need his attention: family, church, work, self, and God. At times he felt his life was out of control. As his coach, I asked if he had a written purpose statement for his life. He had not, and that became his assignment before our next meeting. A week later he sent me an e-mail with his life purpose statement attached. It was very well done and reflected that he had spent a great deal of time thinking and praying through this assignment. Our next session was spent discussing the statement and how he could use it to structure his life.

Managing our lives well requires that we set priorities based on what we believe are the most important tasks we need to accomplish. Few people have taken the time to reflect on what God is calling them to do with their lives and to write it out as a life purpose or vision statement. Many people have some idea of what they want to do with their lives, but a vision that is not thought through and written down is merely a dream. It has little power to guide one through decisions that need to be made. Writing down that life purpose statement, however, helps solidify it in our minds and gives us a valuable tool by which we can compare the merit of all the things that seek our attention. The bivocational pastor I was coaching was allowing a lot of good things to distract him from achieving the most important things. Writing out what he believes God's purposes are for his life allows him to say no to those requests that might be good but are not the best for him right now. Already he is finding ways to spend more time with his family and taking better care of himself by setting aside time each week to do things he enjoys.

The second suggestion I have for persons wanting to better manage their lives is to find a good coach to help in beginning the process. Not only am I coaching other people, but I also have a coach who helps me think through the issues that are challenging me and asks the hard questions that others might not be willing to ask. Some people think having a life coach is too expensive, but actually having a coach is a good investment in your future success and happiness.

The other day I was trying to saw some miter corners with an old miter box and handsaw. Not only was it hard work, but the corners didn't look very good either. Finally I gave in and bought an electric miter saw. Five minutes after taking it out of the box, I had all the boards cut, and the corners perfectly fit each other. The money I spent on the miter saw was an investment, not an expense. It made me more effective, and the end product looks much better than my attempts to saw the corners by hand.

Likewise, coaching is an investment in your future. It can help you address some difficult issues that you might not be willing to share with others. Coaching is sometimes defined as the quickest way to get from where you are to where you want to be, and in today's economy time is money. Many bivocational ministers would benefit from having a life coach to help them address the issues they face in ministry, and a good life coach could help them find solutions to time and life management problems. (If you are interested in learning more about having a coach, please check my website at www.bivocationalministries.com.)

Family Obligations
A story is told of a little boy who kept hanging around his father's study at home. The father was attempting to get some work done and was trying to ignore his son. When the father realized that the boy was not leaving, he stopped his work and asked his son what he wanted. The little boy asked, "Do you get paid a lot of money for what you do?" A little surprised, the father said, "Well, yes, I suppose I do." His son dropped a handful of change on the desk and asked, "This is all the money I've got. How much time with you will this buy me?" The brokenhearted father picked up his son, walked out of his study, closing

the door behind him, and spent the rest of the day playing with his son. Unfortunately, this story could be told of too many pastors, bivocational and fully funded.

Hebron Baptist Church understood that my family was a priority with me. That church had a 150-year history of pastors prior to my going there, and if the Lord tarries, many more pastors will follow me. In contrast, I am the only husband my wife has, and I am the only father our children have. If I pastored the largest church in America and lost my family, I would be a failure as a minister.

Our children are now grown and married with children of their own. They both have moved to other states, but it is my prayer that they will never forget that my wife and I were there supporting them in all their activities. Our daughter ran track and played basketball in junior high and high school. Our son played basketball and baseball. My wife and I missed very few of their games. I spent six years coaching our son's summer baseball teams. We did this despite my working a full-time factory job, pastoring a church, and going to school. It happened because family was a priority for us, and we made time to be involved in our children's lives and activities.

For many years my wife and I have scheduled a regular date night each week. The day might change depending on our work schedules, but there are very few weeks when we do not leave the house for a day or evening and enjoy a nice meal and spend some time shopping or enjoying other activities. Her name is written in my day planner, and if someone calls wanting a meeting with me on that day, I simply tell that person I have another appointment scheduled.

Families should not be shortchanged in the bivocational minister's schedule. They are a key part of your ministry and an even more essential part of your life. They should not be the recipients of your leftover time, assuming you have any; instead, they should be at the top of your priority list.

Many bivocational churches have little to offer their youth. One of my regrets as the pastor of our church was that we never had many youth, which meant that my children did not have the privilege of being involved in a strong youth group. At one time we tried to address this problem by hiring youth ministers to build up that ministry, but this effort failed to produce any long-lasting results. At times I felt my ministry was a hindrance to our children's spiritual development because they could not be involved in a strong youth program that could help them grow in this vital stage of their lives, so we looked for other options they could pursue.

Our daughter and another girl from our church became involved in a youth group that met during the week. Our son also attended some other youth programs during his high school years. Both of them were involved in our church on Sundays but found these opportunities to be involved with others their own age to be beneficial. Some churches would not approve of the pastor's children attending other churches' youth activities, but Hebron never objected.

Every church and pastor will have to address this issue if there are children in the pastor's home. The pastor's children should not be penalized because they attend a small church that cannot offer a good youth program. They must be allowed to involve themselves in activities with other Christian youth as a part of their own spiritual development.

Finances

As reported in chapter 3, some bivocational ministers are paid relatively well while others receive a very small salary. In some situations this is a reflection on the church and its financial limitations, but in many instances bivocational churches pay their ministers very poorly because the minister allows them to do so. Dr. Phil McGraw often says that we teach people how to treat us,[2] and this can certainly be true when it comes to pastoral salaries.

Requesting a larger salary from the church may be difficult for a pastor to do, but churches need to be challenged to pay their ministers a decent salary. Judicatory leaders need to speak up for their bivocational ministers, but it is also the ministers' responsibility to teach their churches that they have a biblical responsibility to provide financially for their ministers (1 Corinthians 9:7-14).

A few years ago judicatory leaders in a western state told me of a strong bivocational church in their area. The church called a new pastor who was financially prosperous. He asked the church not to pay him a salary but to put that money toward ministry. The church grew under his leadership and became used to not paying a minister. The time came when he left the church and they began to seek another pastor. Of course, they could not find one who was willing to serve them with no compensation, yet they refused to call a pastor they had to pay. They now believed that if a pastor was sufficiently spiritual, he or she would not expect to receive a salary for ministry. Unable to find a pastor, the church soon began to decline until it finally closed its doors. The pastor may have thought he was doing the church a favor, but he was sowing seeds that would eventually lead to its destruction. Churches have a responsibility to provide financially for their pastors, and they must be challenged to meet that responsibility.

One way a church and minister can address the issue of finances is to determine the number of units of time the minister will serve the church and pay so much per unit. There are three units of time for each day: morning, afternoon, and evening. This makes for a total of twenty-one units per week. Obviously, under this system Sunday morning would count as one unit, but it is also recommended that an additional unit be paid for sermon preparation. Therefore, Sunday morning would be two units. Sunday evening and midweek services would be additional units. No doubt some units would be expected each week for visitation and administration. It is often recommended that churches pay fifty to one hundred dollars per unit. Simply total up the number of units expected for each week and multiply by the agreed upon amount per unit, and the pastor's salary is determined.

Although this is one way of setting a pastor's salary, it is not my preferred way, because it is very difficult to determine how much time the bivocational minister will spend in ministry each week. It is unlikely that a bivocational minister would refuse to visit a parishioner in the hospital because the number of work units had already been met for the week. I would also hope that church members would not want to reduce the pastor's salary because he or she did not meet the unit expectation during a particular week. My preferred way is to have spiritual, responsible people sit down with the pastor and determine a fair salary package that is acceptable to both the minister and the church.

Other components that make up a pastor's compensation package can add money to the pastor's bank account without costing the church any more money. A parsonage allowance offers the pastor much of her or his salary tax free, but more than half of the bivocational ministers I surveyed reported that they did not receive a parsonage allowance. In fact, many seemed unaware that a housing allowance is an option for ministers. This is an area in which small churches with limited finances can improve the income of their pastor with no additional money. Ministers and churches who want to learn more about the benefits of housing allowances and how to set one up should contact their judicatory leader or accountant.

Benefits

Medical insurance is the largest benefit most churches provide their fully funded pastors, but I have met few bivocational ministers who are provided insurance by their churches. In most cases the other employer or the spouse's employer provides insurance benefits for the bivocational minister and family. But what can be done when neither the church nor the other employer provides medical insurance?

One pastor I know serves a small church and receives no insurance benefits from her other employer. Almost all of her church salary goes to provide insurance benefits for the family. Due to medical issues in the family, it is imperative that they have insurance, and this arrangement works out well for her and for the church.

One benefit I believe is important for a church to provide their pastors is a book allowance. This is usually set up as a reimbursable expense. Good books are expensive, and a church should see this as an investment they are making in their pastor that will return back to them in his or her increased effectiveness. (Hebron once asked me how much I wanted for a book allowance. I told them I would spend whatever they gave me! They decided to leave it at four hundred dollars a year.) When a pastor purchases books, the receipt is submitted to the church treasurer, who writes a check for the amount. As long as careful records and receipts are kept, this money is not considered taxable income.

Along the same line, churches should provide their bivocational minister with a continuing education allowance. There are many conferences and workshops that are beneficial to the ongoing personal and professional growth of the minister. This is another way the church can invest in their future. Some will argue that they are not going to provide training for their pastor because she or he will probably leave their church anyway. Someone has said that the only thing worse than training employees and losing them is not training them and keeping them. The same could be said of pastors.

A more common benefit offered to bivocational ministers is a mileage allowance. Others also receive funds for convention expenses or hospitality. Like allowances for books and continuing education, these may be reimbursable benefits, payable only on submission of appropriate receipts, but they are a great tax-free way for churches to support the ministry of their bivocational leader. Just keep in mind that while parsonage allowances and reimbursements are simple to establish, they must be set up properly or the IRS will disallow them. If the church has questions about how to do this, the treasurer should check with their judicatory leaders or a tax advisor who is familiar with clergy tax matters—including the often challenging expectation of the IRS that clergy pay their taxes on a quarterly basis.

Speaking of the IRS and related matters, I mentioned briefly in chapter 3 the issue of Social Security. More needs to be said on that issue. The IRS considers a pastor as an employee of the church, but Social Security sees the pastor as self-employed. This means the pastor must pay into Social Security at a higher rate. For that reason, many churches are now covering that added expense as a Social Security offset. This money will be taxable income, but it will also reduce the tax bite at the end of the year. Again, I recommend talking to a tax advisor or denominational official who is knowledgeable about how to set this up.

Retirement Planning

Most denominations have some type of pension program for their ministers, but I found that few bivocational ministers who responded to my survey were enrolled in their denomination's program. I served for a number of years as pastor at Hebron before asking the church to enroll me in our denomination's pension program. That request brought about the biggest disagreement we had in the church during my pastorate there. Sides were clearly drawn, and even though the budget that included paying into the pension program was approved, people were still upset, so I asked that the church not immediately enroll me in the program. Since we had not experienced such a disagreement before, I felt that it was important that everyone be heard before moving ahead.

When I met with those who were opposed to enrolling me in the pension program, I found they had three basic arguments: (1) This was not something the church had ever done before. (2) The church could not afford it. (3) Because our program required the church to pay 16 percent of the minister's income into the program, they saw it as a very large pay raise. We addressed each of these arguments, and at our next business meeting, it was brought up for another vote. This time it passed unanimously, and it was never an issue again.

Those who oppose paying into a retirement program for their minister nevertheless have concerns about their own financial well-being during their retirement years. People now live longer, Social Security benefits are less certain, and people need as many financial resources available to them as possible. Therefore, churches, including bivocational churches, need to be responsible to ensure that the retirement years of those who have served them are as comfortable as possible.

If your church is not part of a denomination or does not have a pension program available to them, ask that they pay into an IRA or some other instrument that will provide you and your family with retirement income. I have found *Money* magazine to be an excellent resource for investigating the various retirement programs available today.

Cultural Perceptions
Unfortunately, as I observed early in this volume, some denominations, churches, seminaries, and even other pastors still see bivocational ministry as an inferior form of ministry. Do not be surprised if at times others make you feel—intentionally or not—like a second-class citizen in the kingdom of God. They will wonder why you can't cut it in the real church world, and their attitudes may even affect the way you view yourself and your calling. You must not seek validation for what you are doing from other people.

Only you know what God has called you to do. This sense of calling is key to the bivocational minister overcoming the negative perceptions some have of our ministry. Your sense of self-worth must come from within yourself and from God. Continually remind yourself of what the Word of God says about you and of how God sees you. View the church God has given you to serve as a significant ministry. Regardless of its size, your church is made up of people for whom Jesus Christ died. They need a shepherd who will minister to their needs and lead them in the paths God has laid out. The community in which your church is located is a mission field that needs your church to be a lighthouse that can help guide them into a new relationship with God. The exciting thing about all this is that God has called you, a bivocational minister, to be the person who will be used to provide this ministry and this leadership!

In a very helpful book I often recommend to bivocational ministers, H. B. London Jr. and Neil Wiseman write, "Every assignment is holy ground because Jesus gave Himself for the people who live there. Every place is important because God wants you to accomplish something supernatural there. Every situation is special because ministry is needed there. Like Queen Esther, you have come to the Kingdom for a time like this."[3] Ignore the critics and keep your focus on God and God's call on your life. Rejoice that you are trusted with this awesome responsibility, and make it your purpose to fulfill everything God has called you to do.

Challenges for the Church

Inferiority Complex

A bivocational church must avoid the risk of thinking of itself as an inferior church that cannot afford a fully funded minister. Go into any Christian bookstore today and you will find numerous books that describe various surefire ways of growing your church to become the next megachurch. The inference is that if your church isn't growing, something is seriously wrong with your church and/or your commitment to God.

I am certainly not against churches growing and reaching more people for the kingdom of God, but I am against a mentality that causes some churches to believe that, because they have not been able to grow, they are inferior to other churches or God's back is turned on them. Sometimes a congregation's inability to grow numerically is their own fault because they are too inward focused, but sometimes demographical or other issues make it very difficult for a church to increase its membership. In other cases, a lack of growth may be due to poor leadership in the past. Regardless of the reason, the fact that God has put it in the heart of a person to come as the minister of the church should be reason enough to recognize that the Lord is not through with your congregation. Calling a bivocational minister is not a step backward; it is a step forward toward a better future for the church.

Traditional Views of the Church

The traditional expectation for a church, at least for the last half century, has been that an ordained seminary graduate would devote all of her or his time and energy to leading it. Some church members will find it very difficult to accept that their pastor may not be a seminary graduate, may not be ordained, and will have another job to provide financial support. Many of these churches may have plateaued or been in decline for years and could continue having a fully funded pastor only because they had sufficient savings or a large endowment to draw from or because they used a mortgage-free parsonage as a large part of the salary package. It is also likely that these churches have seen a revolving-door pastorate, with few pastors remaining longer than three years, which is another reason the church has been unable to grow.

As we have already seen, it is becoming increasingly difficult to find pastors to serve these churches, but that doesn't keep pastoral search committees from looking for them. One of my responsibilities is to assist search committees, and every year I upset at least one committee when I tell them it will be difficult to find someone to come as their pastor unless they are willing to consider a bivocational minister.

If these churches do call a bivocational minister, he or she may face a great deal of hostility. The churches become angry that they no longer fit their traditional view of a church, and that anger is then directed at the minister, the person whose presence reminds them of the changes taking place. The minister may find that his or her recommendations are met with resistance. After all, these churches are not convinced that this person is even a valid minister, at least not the kind they have been used to.

Unless these churches are willing to accept the changes that are occurring in ministry and in their churches, it may be counterproductive for them to call a bivocational minister. It is unlikely that a good relationship can be developed if the church is angry that they cannot attract a fully funded pastor. It is unfair to call a minister into such a hostile situation, and it is unlikely that a successful ministry will result. Such churches would be wise to bring in a consultant from their judicatory or a coach to assist them in coming to terms with their situation and helping them discern a new vision from God for their future.

Community Expectations
Calling a bivocational minister may also create questions within the community. Many people in the community, even those who are not involved with a church, share the same traditional expectations regarding pastors that many churches have. They may wonder what is wrong with a church that has to call a factory worker or insurance salesperson as its pastor. If the pastor does not have a seminary degree, people in the community may question whether that person is qualified to preach, conduct weddings and funerals, or lead the church. Persons in the community looking for a church may ignore the one led by a bivocational minister because it doesn't fit their traditional expectations of a church.

Leadership Empowerment
As noted earlier in this book, bivocational churches must have strong lay leaders capable of providing ministry, and some small churches struggle to find good lay leaders. A member of a small

church called the judicatory leader of their denomination asking for his assistance. She named a number of problems in the church and asked if there were any programs or resources that could help them. The judicatory leader suggested that he needed to meet with the church leadership to get their take on the situation and to find out if they were interested in working together to resolve the issues she named. She responded that one of the problems was that the church had no leadership team. The church's own pastor later confirmed that fact and agreed that it was one of the reasons for the church's problems.

A friend of mine was assisting a pastoral search committee as it looked for a new pastor. He asked about the lay leaders, and the committee responded that the church had few persons willing to provide leadership. One man on the committee, who also serves as a deacon, said that the church only had one other deacon and few people willing to assume any leadership responsibilities in the church.

These types of churches often have unrealistic expectations of their pastors. They look for a pastor who will come riding in on a great white horse and save them from all their problems. These are the churches that usually tell me they need a pastor who is a good preacher, who will visit all the church members on a regular basis, and who will grow their youth group because "the youth are the future of the church." They talk about how much they are committed to growth, but many times they are simply committed to watching the pastor grow the church, and if it doesn't happen, they will quickly look to replace the pastor for one who will.

I cannot emphasize enough that the pastor and laity of a bivocational church must be partners in the work. Churches and pastors must agree on what the church needs the pastor to do, and lay leaders must be trained and empowered to do the rest. This will probably require significant training, because training the laity to do ministry has been sorely lacking in many small churches. For too long the mind-set in these churches has been that the pastor is brought in to minister to the church, and the laity are to be recipients of that ministry. If these churches want to experience genuine ministry, the lay leaders must accept the fact that they too are called by God to provide ministry to the church and the community around them.

Pastoral Leadership Issues

Another aspect of leadership empowerment that is a risk to both the church and minister is that some churches are reluctant to give leadership status to their bivocational ministers. Many of these churches have grown used to a revolving-door pastorate and do not expect their pastor to stay very long. They may appreciate the pastor's sermons, personality, and enthusiasm, but they are not going to trust the future of their church to someone who is likely to leave soon. No matter how good her or his ideas may seem, the church knows from experience that by the time these good ideas are implemented, the pastor will probably be gone, and they will be left with trying to do something new that no one has any experience doing. If the new ideas don't work, the future of their church could be in jeopardy, and this is not a risk the church is willing to take. It becomes very difficult in such an environment for the pastor to be given any status in the church as a leader.

This is a risk to the church because it has called this person to be their pastor, and the pastor expected that call to include providing spiritual leadership. Few pastors are willing to remain long in a church that is not interested in following their leadership. I know a pastor who was selected to be involved in a project that would bring transformation to the participating churches. He attended several training events for two years. In the second year of the program, a team from the church was selected to attend the training events with him. The training event leaders, the leadership team, and the pastor developed several recommendations that would help the church develop some new ministries that could lead to new growth in the church. Every recommendation was rejected by the congregation. The church does not know it, but their pastor is now seeking a new place to serve. He simply cannot continue to serve as pastor of a church that is not interested in his leadership. His leaving will be a great loss to the church.

Bivocational Ministry Is Difficult

People who accept the call to be a bivocational minister will face many challenges. Some will question their call, and a few will reject it completely. The bivocational minister will find it difficult to balance all the demands on his or her time. In most situations the salary will be small with few other financial benefits available. The church who calls a bivocational minister will also likely face significant challenges. The good news is that these difficulties can be overcome, and both the minister and church can enjoy a rewarding ministry. That will be our focus of the next chapter.

Recommended Resources

Covey, Stephen R., A. Roger Merrill, and Rebecca R. Merrill. *First Things First: To Live, to Love, to Learn, to Leave a Legacy.* New York: Simon & Schuster, 1994.

Dorr, Luther M. *The Bivocational Pastor.* Nashville: Broadman, 1988.

Howard, J. Grant. *Balancing Life's Demands: A New Perspective on Priorities.* Sisters, OR: Multnomah, 1994.

London, H. B., Jr., and Neil B. Wiseman. *Pastors at Greater Risk: Real Help for Pastors from Pastors Who've Been There.* Ventura: Regal, 2003.

———. *Your Pastor Is an Endangered Species.* Wheaton: Victor, 1996.

Mace, David, and Vera Mace. *What's Happening to Clergy Marriages?* Nashville: Abingdon, 1980.

Swenson, Richard A. *Margin: Restoring Emotional, Physical, Financial, and Time Reserves to Overloaded Lives.* Colorado Springs: NavPress, 1992.

CHAPTER 6

What Makes Bivocational Ministry Rewarding?

Many of us who serve as bivocational ministers believe the rewards of being bivocational far outweigh the difficulties of this form of ministry. These rewards exist for both the bivocational minister and the church he or she serves. In the first section of this chapter, we will examine some of the benefits of being a bivocational minister, and in the second section, we will look at the benefits that exist for the church.

Benefits to the Minister

Flexibility

Listing flexibility as a benefit may seem strange after discussing in earlier chapters the time constraints most bivocational ministers feel; nevertheless, most bivocational ministers do find that their ministries are less structured than those of fully funded pastors. In the small churches served by bivocational ministers, there is less administrative work to do, fewer services each week for which to prepare messages, fewer committees and boards to meet with, and less expectation that regular office hours be kept. During my twenty-year pastorate, I had some weeks when I spent forty or more hours doing church work and other weeks when I didn't spend more than ten hours in ministry-related activities.

One fully funded minister I know was asked to leave his church in part because he struggled to keep regular office hours. He is more of an evangelist than an administrator, and he preferred being with people to working in an office. After leaving that church, he found other employment and began a bivocational pastorate. He is much happier with the flexibility he now feels and is enjoying a successful ministry. It is unlikely he would ever return to a fully funded ministry.

Note that flexibility does require the minister to be a self-motivator. There are no time cards to punch, and generally bivocational churches will not track the hours their minister is involved in ministry. Most bivocational ministers I know are hardworking individuals who pour their hearts into their ministry, but I also know a few who just show up on Sunday, preach a sermon, and collect a check. Their churches are not well served, and such people should either reexamine their call or leave the ministry. Having a more flexible schedule is a great benefit to the bivocational minister, but it is one that must not be abused.

Use of Multiple Gifts and Callings
Some bivocational ministers are called into this form of ministry after spending years in other occupations. As we saw in chapter 3, bivocational ministers are involved in various other types of careers, and many of them would say that they feel called to those careers just as they feel called to ministry. In fact, many of them would go so far as to say that their other careers are also ministries to which God has called them. Southern Baptist bivocational ministers have long considered themselves to be "double-duty, twice blessed" individuals who believe that God has called them to both vocations.

Expanded Ministry Opportunities
Christians can become rather isolated within their own little circles of church life. It is possible to spend all of one's time

listening to Christian radio, watching Christian television programs, reading Christian novels and magazines, and gathering together with like-minded folk two to four times a week and seldom have any contact with the unchurched community. One small church held an "Invite a Friend Sunday," and no one brought any friends! As they reflected on what happened, one longtime member of the church admitted she had no non-Christian friends. Others in the church identified the same reality in their lives. Not only is this true for laity, but it is also often true of clergy. Many pastors would be hard-pressed to identify more than a handful, if that many, of non-Christian friends. That means much of their ministry is limited to church members and others who attend their services. This is not usually the case for the bivocational minister.

One minister recently told me that one of the benefits he enjoys as a bivocational minister is the contact he has with a wide variety of people. As a salesperson, he calls on several businesses, and he has been able to develop relationships with many of the people he serves. In his twenty-five years as a bivocational minister, he has had the opportunity to pray with and minister to a wide variety of people, some of whom would be unlikely to attend the church he pastors. He has a ministry opportunity that stretches far beyond his church.

Roots in the Community
Many bivocational ministers serve in communities in which they may have lived for many years. When I became pastor at Hebron, our family did not have to move, our children did not have to change school districts, and we did not have to develop new friendships. Hebron was located in the same county our family had lived in virtually all our lives. One of the things I told the search committee was that I may not have the education and experience other pastors had, but I did know where the hospital was located, and I had traveled the roads where most of the congregation lived.

Being able to serve in the community in which the bivocational minister's family already lives provides a measure of stability to the family that a fully funded pastor cannot always provide. It is not unusual for fully funded pastors to change churches every three to five years, which usually means that the family must move. Children are taken out of the school districts where they have been attending and are obliged to make all new friends in unfamiliar surroundings. Families must find new doctors, dentists, banks, and other service providers after they move.

When our son began high school, he became concerned that I might take another church and move before he completed school. He wanted to stay in the school system he had attended all his life, because that is where his friends were, and he wanted to be involved in the sports programs in the school. My wife and I prayed about his concerns, and I felt the freedom to assure him that we would not move until he completed high school. It was much easier for me to make that promise as a bivocational minister because our income and standard of living were not based on my church salary. He felt reassured and was able to enjoy his high school years without having to worry about moving.

Increased Income

As reported in chapter 3, most bivocational ministers do not receive a large salary, but since that salary is not their only income, they may enjoy a higher standard of living than their fully funded counterparts. In some cases this dual income arrangement allows the bivocational minister to purchase a home and enjoy all the rewards of home ownership, including the opportunity to build equity in the home. By owning a home, the minister qualifies for a parsonage allowance that shelters some of her or his income from federal income tax. This results in more income to the minister without any additional cost to the church.

Having more than one source of income can also allow the

minister more flexibility in her or his ministry. Before entering the ministry, I had a conversation with our pastor about a particular doctrine. He admitted he agreed with me but said he could not preach that in our church or he would probably be fired. He lived in the church parsonage and had a wife and children to consider. Being bivocational gave me more freedom, for which I have always been thankful. Even if the church dismissed me, our family would still have a roof over our heads and food on the table.

Appreciation by the Church
I enjoyed a wonderful relationship with my church. That doesn't mean that we did not have occasional disagreements and have to work through some issues, but during my twenty-year pastorate, I felt appreciated and loved by the church. One of the things that kept me from thinking too hard about seeking another place to serve was that I knew of too many horror stories of pastors who did not receive the kind of appreciation I enjoyed from the congregation at Hebron. The grass is not always greener on the other side of the fence.

Church members remembered my birthday and our anniversary. We could count on receiving numerous cards at Christmastime. The church held celebrations on my tenth anniversary at the church and when I graduated from Bible school and college. Some of the church members attended our daughter's wedding even though it was in another state. Most of them attended our twenty-fifth wedding anniversary party. They honored my wife by giving her gifts at special occasions. We frequently were told how much our ministry was appreciated.

My experience is not unusual for bivocational ministers. That may be one reason why so many report high satisfaction in their work. Our churches do seem to appreciate the ministry we provide, and they are not reluctant to let us know their appreciation. As difficult as the work can become at times, that appreciation makes it all worthwhile. Someone once said he could go a month on one sincere compliment, and I know exactly how he feels.

Benefits to the Church

Longer Pastorates

Pastors do not automatically begin leading a church simply because of their position. Congregations, especially small ones, have to trust the pastor before allowing him or her to become a leader in the church, and building that trust takes time. They have to observe his or her character over the long haul to ensure that words and actions are aligned. This requires that the pastor remain at the church long enough to earn the trust of the congregation before they can be expected to follow the pastor's leadership.

In chapter 5 we talked about the need for lay leadership training. One of the reasons lay leaders seldom receive the training they need is because such training does take time, and many pastors are not willing to invest that amount of time in such training. Many pastors never unpack their boxes when they come to serve a small church. They know they will not be there long, and they are unwilling to make any plans that will take more than a year or two to complete. Lay leadership training must be ongoing in a church that is serious about having all its members involved in ministry, so these pastors never even start such training because they know they will not be there long enough to enjoy the benefits. Small churches have suffered much from such shortsighted thinking. Only when a pastor intends to remain at a church for an extended period of time is lay leader training likely to happen.

Moreover, long pastorates are unlikely in small churches unless the pastor is bivocational. There are a number of reasons for this, with the primary reason being financial.[1] It is sufficient here to say that small churches are unlikely to enjoy a successful ministry unless they are able to keep a pastor for an extended period of time.

Stronger Lay Ministry

Once lay leaders are trained for ministry, they must be challenged to become involved in ministry. Until his recent retirement, Leon Wilson served as national missionary for bivocational ministries in the Southern Baptist Convention. Prior to that ministry, he was the bivocational pastor of a six-hundred-member church in Oklahoma City, a church he began in his home with thirteen persons. This church had six staff ministers, all of whom were also bivocational by choice. Wilson and his staff believed that the reason the church grew under their intentional bivocational leadership was that laity were more involved in ministry. In fact, Wilson believes, "It's a crime for someone to fully fund a staff and take away church members' ministry."[2]

Fully funded pastors, especially in small churches, often complain they feel like a "hired gun." They are brought into the church to provide ministry while the church members sit back and enjoy their services. Such an attitude is not only unbiblical (see Ephesians 4:11-16), it also leads to clergy burnout and limited growth of the church and its members.

Members of bivocational churches understand that their pastor has a second job that requires a certain amount of time, and they are much more likely to be involved in ministry. It was not uncommon for me to learn that a church member was in the hospital and go to visit that person only to find out that others from the church had already been there. Seeing the church ministering to one another in that way was a joy.

The wise bivocational minister will spend time teaching on spiritual gifts and encouraging church members to identify areas of ministry in which they can use their God-given gifts. Further-more, he or she will give these members "permission" to minister. In some churches, previous pastors may have discouraged lay ministry,

Challenges and Opportunities of Bivocational Ministry

believing that ministry was limited to ordained persons, and in these churches, letting the members know that God has uniquely equipped each of them to do ministry is vital. Offering to train and resource persons who want to become more involved in lay ministry is also essential. Do not assume that people will come to you and ask to receive such training. The minister is responsible to approach laypeople, challenge them to become involved in some aspect of ministry in the church, and offer to train them for that ministry. I learned late in my pastoral ministry that many people wanted to be more involved but were waiting for me to fulfill my pastoral responsibility to train and equip them for ministry. My failure in this area had limited our ministry effectiveness for many years.

More Money Available for Ministry

Finances are tight in most churches, especially in small ones. Small churches trying to support a fully funded pastor will find that a huge percentage of their income will go toward salary and benefits. With the rising costs of insurance, that percentage will only increase. For most small churches, the cost of pastoral salaries and benefits are the single largest expense in their budget, followed by the cost of maintaining their buildings. What money remains is primarily spent on programming for the church members, leaving little money available for outreach or ministry in the community. Such churches are stuck in a maintenance mode, unable to have much impact in the community.

Calling a bivocational minister can free up substantial amounts of money for a more effective outreach into the community. A bivocational minister will often have insurance provided by her or his other employer, eliminating that expense for the church. The church may be able to offer a reduced salary as well, making more money available for ministry. Too many small churches that have considered themselves full-time have been paying part-time wages, causing great financial strain on their pastors. In such cases these pastors' salaries probably should not be reduced.

However, even in these churches, having a bivocational minister will likely make more money available for ministry.

New Church Plants

In the early 1980s I was sitting in class at the Bible school I attended when we were asked by a denominational leader if any of us would be interested in starting new churches in an adjoining state. After he explained their plans to start several new churches in one particular city, I asked if they would use bivocational ministers as new church planters. He quickly informed us that new church planting was not work for bivocational people because it took a lot of dedicated effort to start a new church, and bivocational ministers could not put forth the effort and time to be effective. I'm glad to say that twenty-five years later that theory has largely been proved false by bivocational church planters such as Leon Wilson and others. Today approximately one-third of Southern Baptist new church plants are started by bivocational ministers.[3] Virtually all the new churches started in our region are led by bivocational ministers.

Many denominations are involved in new church planting efforts, and many local churches are committed to starting sister churches in nearby communities and even across the country. These denominations and churches find that funding is a major challenge to their efforts, and a major portion of that funding is for the salary and benefits of the church planter. With bivocational church planters, the money available for new church starts can stretch further and more new churches can be planted.

Another significant benefit the bivocational minister brings to new church planting is that in many cases he or she is indigenous to the area and already familiar with the customs, traditions, and preferences of the community. The locally grown church planter is not apt to be seen as an outsider brought in to start a new church, but rather as a person who is "one of us" and can be trusted. The new church may actually start from the friendships the planter has developed over the years through his or her employment and other involvement in the community. This can lead to a more effective new church plant and make its success more likely.

Bivocational Ministry Is Very Rewarding

Bivocational ministers and the churches they serve often find that this ministry is very rewarding. Ministers are often able to serve in communities in which they already live, eliminating the need to uproot their families. Their other employment provides a mission field for their ministry. Although the salaries paid to bivocational ministers is typically low, when it is added to their other income they may enjoy a higher standard of living than their fully funded counterparts. The roots they have in the community and their financial stability often means that they are less likely to seek other places to serve, and the church benefits from longer pastorates. The church also has more money available for ministries to the community as it does not have to spend so much of its money on a pastor's salary and benefits. Bivocational ministry is truly a "win-win" for the minister and the church.

Recommended Resources

Bickers, Dennis. *The Bivocational Pastor: Two Jobs, One Ministry*. Kansas City, MO: Beacon Hill, 2004.

———. *The Tentmaking Pastor: The Joy of Bivocational Ministry*. Grand Rapids: Baker, 2000.

Borden, Paul D. *Hit the Bullseye: How Denominations Can Aim the Congregation at the Mission Field*. The Convergence eBook Series. Edited by Tom Bandy and Bill Easum. Nashville: Abingdon, 2003.

Stetzer, Ed. *Planting Missional Churches: Planting a Church That's Biblically Sound and Reaching People in Culture*. Nashville: Broadman & Holman, 2006.

PART FOUR

Bivocational Ministry in Action

CHAPTER 7

What Is a Week in the Life of a Bivocational Minister?

Because bivocational ministers have so many different types of jobs in addition to their ministries, it is very difficult to describe a typical week. During much of my pastorate, I worked forty hours a week in a factory. My work schedule was set and could not be varied. If I needed to conduct a funeral service or attend a continuing education event, I had to take an unpaid, unexcused absence or a vacation day. Since unexcused absences could lead to termination, I normally took a vacation day.

After I took early retirement from the factory job, our family took ownership of a heating and air-conditioning company. My work schedule became much more flexible. My plan was to work at our business until lunch each day and then focus on ministry responsibilities during the afternoon hours. If ministry needs arose earlier in the day, I could tend to them without worrying about losing my job. If my pastoral responsibilities were heavier than usual, I simply didn't go into our company at all that day. Obviously, the more flexible the schedule one has, the easier it is to serve as a bivocational minister.

Balancing the Demands

After a short while as a bivocational pastor, I decided I wanted to pursue an education that would enable me to be a better minister. I enrolled at Boyce Bible School in Louisville, Kentucky. Although it was only a two-year program, it took me four years to complete it because I could attend classes only part-time. During this time I had to work the night shift in the factory so I could attend the classes Boyce offered.

Following graduation from that program, I enrolled at a university to work on a bachelor's degree. Because I was working full-time and pastoring a church, I could take only a few classes each semester, and this degree took me seven years to complete. To help the reader better understand how bivocational ministers juggle various responsibilities, I will share a typical week of those college years. Although I continued to work the night shift during part of those years, I will use my schedule after I transferred back to the day shift. There is nothing normal about working nights!

On Sunday morning I would usually be at the church by 8:00. Our Sunday school started at 9:30, and a worship service followed at 10:30. I taught the young adult class in addition to preaching. Sunday afternoons were spent with family or studying, and we would return to church that evening around 6:00 for the evening service.

Since I was working the day shift during this time, I would clock in by 7:00 A.M. and work until 3:30 P.M. Monday through Friday. I typically carried three classes each semester, with each class meeting one night a week for two-and-a-half hours. Most classes started at 7:00 P.M., so if the classes met in my hometown, I had about three hours to clean up, eat dinner, and study or do church work. The university I attended offered several classes each semester in our community, but once I took those, I had to drive an hour each way to the campus. That shrank my evening hours and caused me to return home even later at night.

During this time our daughter was in college and our son was in high school. Our daughter often came home on weekends so we could spend time with her. Our son played on the basketball and baseball teams. Surprisingly enough, I missed very few of his games.

The evenings when I did not have classes or ball games to attend I spent working on sermons, doing church visitation, or doing homework. Every two or three days I would drive out to the church to get the mail and take care of necessary administrative duties. As the pastor of a church, I was always on call, especially when our church members were ill or in the hospital. Going to the hospital to visit someone on my way to class was not uncommon.

Fitting Family into the Schedule

Although we were involved in our children's activities, my wife and I had little time for ourselves. It was during this time that we committed to a date night each week, usually on Friday evenings. As I have shared in many sermons and workshops, more important than what we do on those dates is that we are together. It is a time to talk and just be with each other away from all distractions. To ensure we have no distractions, we normally go about an hour from the house to get away from the telephones, computers, and the possibility of someone dropping by to visit.

Some people cannot get away from the telephone because they carry a cell phone everywhere they go. I normally have one with me as well, but my cell phone is for my convenience, not so others can contact me anytime they feel like it. My wife, our two children, and our regional office have the number to my cell phone. I usually leave it in the car when I go into a meeting, and I always leave it in the car when my wife and I go out to eat. This is our time, and I do not intend for our time to be interrupted by my phone ringing every time we start to talk. The only exception to this rule is if one of our children is traveling or someone in the family is sick.

Part of managing one's life and maintaining balance is managing the cell phone. I overheard someone ask one time what people did before they had cell phones, and the answer given was that they had a life. Cell phones are great tools, but they have to be managed if you want to have a life. Turn yours off and enjoy some family time.

Fitting God into the Schedule

Throughout my ministry, the one thing that has always been a struggle is spending time with God. While attending Bible school, I first noticed that although I was learning a lot about God, I wasn't spending a lot of time with God. In conversations with other students, I found that they shared the same difficulty. At various times in my ministry, I have realized that my prayer and devotional life was not what it should be. In sharing this problem with other bivocational and fully funded ministers, I have found that I am not alone. Spending time with God is something we ministers constantly have to address.

Effective ministry must flow out of who we are. If we do not grow deeper in our relationship with God, how can we expect to help others grow deeper in theirs? Spiritually shallow pulpits lead to spiritually shallow churches. Moreover, our own spiritual well-being requires that we make time for God in our schedules. God loves us and wants to spend time with us. We need to spend time in prayer, Bible reading, and meditation so that we can experience that love in fresh ways and so that our faith can grow. Psalm 42:1 says, "As the deer pants for streams of water, so my soul pants for you, O God." May that be the prayer and desire of every believer and especially those of us who serve in ministry.

Fitting Self into the Schedule

Even more difficult has been taking the time to care for myself. Shortly after graduating from Bible school, I experienced a major clinical depression that was caused by exhaustion. During those four years, I seldom slept more than three hours a day. I was living on adrenaline, and when I graduated the adrenaline ran out. The brain chemicals were depleted, and even thinking clearly became a challenge. I was able to pastor and work, but my body basically shut down to all other activities. I spent a year on medication and counseling before I began to function normally again. It was an experience I never want to repeat.

I had always boasted that I would rather burn out than rust out. I wasn't smart enough to realize that either way I would be out. God did not create us for nonstop activity, and living that way is poor stewardship of the gifts and calling the Lord has given us. I find that many ministers live on the edge of exhaustion. We seem to take great pleasure in our busy schedules and hectic lives. While this is true of both bivocational and fully funded ministers, I find it especially true of those of us in bivocational leadership. I think back to times when I wanted people to know how busy I was for the kingdom of God, and I enjoyed the accolades people gave me for my faithfulness and hard work. As a result, I lost a year of my life to depression, and even worse, I was living a life that God never intended me to live.

Author and medical doctor Richard Swenson understands the need to rest, and he understands the temptation many of us feel to overextend ourselves. In a book that every bivocational minister should be required to read, he writes:

> God, however, has commanded us to rest. A biblically authentic and balanced life will include time to be still, to remember, to meditate, to delight in who He is and what He has made. But a large obstacle stands in our way: There is no glory in rest. No social acclaim. We are never a hero because we rest. We can only be still and better wait upon the Lord. We can only meditate upon the Word more. We can only have more margin with which to serve our neighbor. These things, however, are not socially reimbursable.[1]

One of the lessons I learned during my depression was that if I did not take care of myself, I would not be able to take care of other people. My family suffered, as did our church. I could still function, but at a much lower level, and no one received the care he or she deserved. Because I know that I will always have a tendency to be a workaholic and overextend myself, I intentionally make time to relax, recharge, and reconnect with my family and with God.

For me this usually involves spending some time at the gym several days a week, playing a round of golf every week or two, taking rides on my motorcycle, and playing with our new puppy. It also means that my wife and I protect our weekly date time. This summer we have spent a lot of time on our deck during the evening hours, sitting in rocking chairs reading and talking.

You have to find what helps you relax and schedule time to do those things. Saying that you will do them when you have time is not enough, because you will never have time. As a bivocational minister, you will always be attending to someone who wants your time. You have to manage your time or others will manage it for you, and you will feel like a puppet on a string, always being pulled in one direction or another but never having any time just for yourself. You are the only person who can ensure that you remain healthy spiritually, emotionally, and physically.

Some will argue that this sounds very selfish, but it isn't. In fact, it is the very reason God gave us the Sabbath. "Remember the Sabbath day by keeping it holy. Six days you shall labor and do all your work, but the seventh day is a Sabbath to the LORD your God" (Exodus 20:8-10). Keeping an entire day as a sabbath may be nearly impossible for most bivocational ministers, but the principle is one we can follow. God has called us to take specific times to rest and reconnect with our families and with the Lord our God. Our health and well-being require it.

Some will protest that they are simply too busy to take blocks of time out for themselves. Such protests mean that you are busier than Jesus was and that your work is more important than his. The multitudes followed Jesus everywhere he went, seeking various healings and other miracles and wanting to hear his teachings, and he often met their needs, but we also read that he sometimes withdrew by himself to pray and rest (see Matthew 14:23; Mark 1:35). In Mark 6:31 he asked his disciples to find a quiet place to rest because of the work they were doing and the continued needs of the people. Jesus modeled for all who serve the importance of taking time to rest and reconnect with God. We require this rest not only for our own well-being, but to be more effective ministers.

We ministers will always have a tendency to overextend ourselves. We are in the ministry because we believe God has called us to care for others, and it is very difficult to say no to people we want to serve. But we must say no to some things in order to have time for the best things. If we do not control our lives and maintain balance between all the things we are expected to do, life will soon get out of control and ministry will become drudgery. Bivocational ministers must find others to assist them in their work so that they have time for the other important aspects of their lives.

Forming Leadership Teams

If I returned to pastoral ministry, one of the first things I would do would be to identify the ministry needs in the church and then form teams to address those needs. Worship would be one of the first things on my list. Developing a worship service that will encourage everyone to experience God should be a top priority. In too many small churches I visit, it appears that the worship service was thrown together about five minutes before everyone else arrived. There is no flow, no continuity, and seemingly little purpose except to sing a few songs and have a sermon. I would want a worship team that could work with me to develop the services at least a month in advance. That means I would have to plan my preaching schedule out at least that far—no Saturday night specials—and share that schedule with the team so we could discuss the sermon themes and develop worship services around them.

I would form a shepherding team as well. In my denomination, that might include the deacons, although it would not have to be limited to them. Before accepting the call to pastoral ministry, I served as a deacon in a church that used a deacon family ministry plan. Each deacon was given a number of families for which he was responsible. We visited, sent cards, and kept in regular contact with our families. It was not uncommon for them to call us when they had questions or needed prayer. If their concerns were serious, we would take them to the pastor, who would then contact them. This freed up the pastor's time while still providing ministry to the family. While I was pastor at Hebron, our deacons used this system to provide excellent care for our members.

A third team a bivocational pastor needs is a strategic planning team. Too many small churches are willing to continually repeat yesterday, never realizing that the needs of their surrounding community may be rapidly changing. This team would be responsible for working closely with the pastor to better understand the needs of the community, the existing ministries the church offers, and the core values and giftedness of the church members, and from that information begin a discernment process to capture God's vision for the future of the church. This team could then assist the pastor in conveying that vision to the members of the church, assisting in the implementation of the vision, and evaluating the effectiveness of any changes that might occur in the church's ministries. Aubrey Malphurs has written an excellent book to guide the work of this team.[2]

A fourth team that would be invaluable to the bivocational minister is a prayer partner team. When John Maxwell became the pastor of Skyline Wesleyan Church in 1981, he soon met a man by the name of Bill Klassen who told Maxwell that he felt led to become his prayer partner. That prayer ministry grew until Maxwell had 120 prayer partners in the church. He attributes the exciting ministry he has enjoyed since those days to his prayer partners. His book *Partners in Prayer* describes how a pastor can develop a prayer partnership in his or her church.[3]

Although my numbers were much smaller than Maxwell's, I enjoyed a similar experience at Hebron. Three of our lay leaders went with me to the Promise Keepers event in Washington, D.C., in 1997. On our way home after the event, these men shared with me their desire to begin to pray for me each Sunday evening prior to our evening worship service. For the next four years until I resigned from the church, five to eight individuals would meet with me in one of our Sunday school rooms and pray for me, my wife, and our church. These prayers had a powerful effect on me and on the church, and we saw some of our most productive ministry during that time. A prayer partner team will be a valuable asset to your church and to your ministry.

You may find other teams to be necessary, depending on the situations that exist in your church, but it seems that these four teams would be important for every church. They would remove some of the workload from the bivocational pastor, provide additional minds and hands with which to address the ministry needs of the church, and surround the pastor with their prayers and support.

Teams or Committees

At this point some readers may be wondering about the difference between committees and teams. While there are many different ways to explain the differences, the primary difference is that committees are involved in the maintenance work of the church while teams are focused on ministry tasks.

A nominating committee is responsible for finding persons willing to serve in various leadership and teaching positions in the church. This is work that needs to be done each year in many churches. The finance committee is often charged with preparing a budget for the upcoming year, and in some churches it is responsible for ensuring that the church's funds are spent according to the budget. Both of these committees and numerous other ones in the church are focused on maintaining the church in an orderly fashion.

The teams referred to earlier are focused on ministry issues: worship, congregational care, and the future direction of the church. The persons on these teams should be carefully selected for their giftedness, their willingness to serve, their ability to accept change, and their close relationship with God. In an ideal situation, the pastor should have great freedom to select the persons for these teams, but in small family churches, the dynamics are often such that he or she may not have complete freedom to do that.

Leadership Development

A bivocational minister should not expect to find lay leaders who are capable of serving on leadership teams without investing time and energy in training them. Certainly there will be some exceptions, but these exist only because some minister prior to you has already done the training.

Many laypeople want to be more involved in the church's ministry in the community and are just waiting to be asked. Reluctant to seem pushy and not wanting to interfere with the pastor, these persons are unlikely to volunteer to accept a key role in the church, but they are praying that some day they will be asked to be involved in some aspect of the church's ministry.

Others are waiting to be challenged with an important assignment. Too often we approach people, promising that this task won't take too much of their time if they will only agree to do it. A nominating committee once asked a person if she would accept a position and assured her that she wouldn't have to do anything except attend an occasional meeting. The woman refused because she didn't want to waste her time with something that did not require anything from her. She was waiting to be challenged to use her gifts and energy in a significant ministry in the church. Busy people are willing to accept ministry responsibilities if they are asked and if they believe that these responsibilities will make a difference in the life of the church or in the lives of other people. But there is one other requirement that must be met if they are to be effective: they must be trained.

Leadership development is not only key to a more effective church; it is key to the bivocational minister being able to enjoy a more balanced life and ministry. Ministers need to identify those persons in their congregations who want to be used of God and begin to pour their lives into these people. If you want prayer partners, teach them how to pray. If you want people to help you identify future direction for the church, teach them how to dream and seek God's guidance. If you want people to assist you in providing care for the church, teach them how to do that. Take them with you to the hospitals and nursing homes. Look for opportunities and resources that will enable you to train your leadership.

In *The Healthy Small Church* I briefly describe how I provided leadership training in our church.[4] There are other ways to do it, but above all you must be intentional about providing it. Two months before I introduced the training in our church, I told the church what was coming and explained why I felt it was necessary to present the training in a certain format. They knew they would be challenged to greater ministry involvement, but they also knew I was serious about providing whatever training and resources they needed. It was a very rewarding time for our church, and it did lead to greater involvement by several people.

Do not be afraid to hold these lay leaders accountable. Many of your laypeople are used to being evaluated by their supervisors at their jobs and will not be offended by a fair evaluation of how they are performing their assignments at church. In fact, many of them will appreciate the opportunity of knowing how well they are doing and how they can improve. Jill Hudson has written an excellent book, *When Better Isn't Enough*, that provides tools churches can use to evaluate the work of the pastor, other staff persons, and volunteers in the church. In an appendix of her book, she gives examples of questions that can be used to measure the twelve characteristics of an effective minister. Then she revises these questions so they can be used for lay volunteers.[5] Many churches will find these evaluation tools helpful, and using them stresses how serious the church is in providing excellent lay ministry to the church family and to the community.

Bivocational ministry is demanding and difficult work, and life can get out of balance rather quickly. But it is very rewarding ministry if the church is willing to partner in ministry with the pastor. The leadership must be willing to become involved in ministry and not rely entirely on the pastor to provide all the ministry to the church, and the pastor must be committed to working with laypeople and training them for the tasks God has called them to do. This kind of partnership can have a significant impact on the church, the community, and the ability of the minister to enjoy a balanced and meaningful life.

Recommended Resources

Baker, Don, and Emery Nester. *Depression: Finding Hope and Meaning in Life's Darkest Shadow*. Portland, OR: Multnomah, 1983.

Barna, George. *The Power of Team Leadership: Finding Strength in Shared Responsibility*. Colorado Springs: WaterBrook, 2001.

Foster, Richard J. *Celebration of Discipline: The Path to Spiritual Growth*. Revised edition. New York: Harper & Row, 1988.

Gangel, Kenneth O. *Team Leadership in Christian Ministry: Using Multiple Gifts to Build a Unified Vision.* Chicago: Moody, 1997.

Gottman, John. *Why Marriages Succeed or Fail: And How You Can Make Yours Last.* New York: Simon and Schuster, 1994.

Hart, Archibald D. *Coping with Depression in the Ministry and Other Helping Professions.* Dallas: Word, 1984.

Howard, J. Grant. *Balancing Life's Demands: A New Perspective on Priorities.* Sisters, OR: Multnomah, 1994.

Howell, John C. *Christian Marriage: Growing in Oneness.* Nashville: Convention Press, 1983.

Jones, Jeffrey D. *Traveling Together: A Guide for Disciple-Forming Congregations.* Herndon, VA: Alban Institute, 2006.

Mace, David and Vera Mace. *What's Happening to Clergy Marriages?* Nashville: Abingdon, 1980.

Maxwell, John C. *The 17 Indisputable Laws of Teamwork: Embrace Them and Empower Your Team.* Nashville: Nelson, 2001.

———. *Today Matters: 12 Daily Practices to Guarantee Tomorrow's Success.* New York: Warner Faith, 2004.

Morgan, Donald W. *Share the Dream, Build the Team: Ten Keys for Revitalizing Your Church.* Grand Rapids: Baker, 2001.

Peterson, Eugene H. *The Contemplative Pastor: Returning to the Art of Spiritual Direction.* Grand Rapids: Eerdmans, 1989.

———. *Working the Angles: The Shape of Pastoral Integrity.* Grand Rapids: Eerdmans, 1987.

Swindoll, Charles R. *Strike the Original Match: Rekindling and Preserving Your Marriage Fire.* Minneapolis: World Wide Publications, 1980.

CHAPTER 8

How Does Bivocational Ministry Work in the Church?

This chapter will examine how various traditions embrace bivocational ministry and what expectations they have for its future. I have not attempted to include every tradition that uses bivocational ministers, only some that are representative of the ways many denominations view and use bivocational leadership. Several of the traditions described here recognize their need for more bivocational ministers but struggle with how to identify, affirm, train, and use these ministers to their fullest potential. One thing that will be apparent by the end of the chapter is that there is a growing need in the United States for bivocational ministers.

American Baptist Churches USA (ABCUSA)

Since 1981 I have served as a bivocational minister in the American Baptist Churches USA. For the first twenty years, I was pastor of Hebron Baptist Church near Madison, Indiana, and since 2001 I have served as an area resource minister for the American Baptist Churches of Indiana and Kentucky. During a good portion of my ministry, I felt like an outsider in the denomination. Part of the problem was my fault. I knew few other bivocational ministers, and I had little time for association activities and even less time for regional and denominational events. The events I did attend seemed to have little value for the ministry I was doing, and I came away feeling that my ministry was second-class at best. Fortunately, this all began to change during my last few years as a pastor.

Our region noticed the good work that was occurring among their bivocational ministers and correctly understood that bivocational ministry was the best option for many of our churches. The Ministers Council of the ABCUSA started an outreach to the bivocational ministers of the denomination called BivoNet, which produced a newsletter titled *Vital Churches* to address the needs and concerns of bivocational ministers. Other regions within the ABCUSA also discovered that bivocational ministry was growing within their regions and that they needed to find new ways to identify those called to this ministry and new ways to train those who did not have formal seminary training. Some have assigned staff persons to specifically relate to their bivocational ministers and find ways to meet their needs. Bivocational ministry is rapidly becoming better accepted in the ABCUSA, and many in judicatory leadership are intentionally challenging men and women within the denomination to consider if they might be called of God to this form of ministry.

Recognizing that their churches need trained bivocational leadership, a few regions have developed training programs for those leaders who have not had the opportunity to graduate from college and seminary. The American Baptist Churches of Indiana and Kentucky developed a program called the Church Leadership Institute in 2002 to provide training for both lay leaders and persons called to bivocational ministry. The program offers two tracks of study. Track one consists of eight courses that can be completed in two years. Graduates of this track earn a certificate in church leadership. The second track includes an additional five courses that are designed for men and women in bivocational ministry, for those who are considering such ministry, and for lay leaders who want to learn more about ministry. Those who

90

complete this track receive a diploma in pastoral ministry. In the spring of 2006, the first diploma class graduated, with seventeen persons receiving their diplomas. Four of these seventeen are now serving as bivocational ministers within the region. More than one hundred students are now enrolled in this program, and plans are being made to offer these classes at a second site that will make the program more accessible to potential students in northern Indiana. Similar programs in every region would enhance the ministry skills and biblical knowledge of the bivocational ministers throughout this denomination.

There is still much work to be done. One issue that the ABCUSA must address is the educational standard for recognized ordination. Our denomination requires the master of divinity as the minimum education standard for ordination, and many bivocational ministers do not have that degree. While our polity does permit a local church ordination to occur in such circumstances, this education standard sends a mixed message to those considering bivocational ministry. Although we talk about the growing need for bivocational ministers in our denomination, we send the message that due to our ordination standards, those persons will be seen as second-class ministers not worthy of full ordination status. In the interest of editorial honesty, I should mention here that I have a local church ordination due to the fact that I do not possess a master of divinity. This has seldom bothered me personally, but it does greatly concern me for others who are called to bivocational ministry but are made to feel as if they are not worthy of full denominational recognition.

A second area the ABCUSA needs to address is that it really does not know much about its bivocational ministers. Few are members of the ministers' council, and even fewer have a profile on file with personnel services. No one in the denominational headquarters in Valley Forge, Pennsylvania, was able to provide me with figures on the numbers of bivocational ministers in the ABCUSA. Prior to sending my 2004 survey to the bivocational ministers in the ABCUSA, I requested contact information from each of the thirty-six regions in the denomination. Only half of those regions replied with the names and addresses of their bivocational ministers. One can only assume the others simply did not know who should receive the survey in their region. A great need exists within the ABCUSA to identify bivocational ministers so that it can better address their needs and develop processes that will enable them to serve more effectively.

Southern Baptist Convention (SBC)

The largest Protestant denomination in America anticipates that bivocational ministers will outnumber their fully funded pastors within the next few years.[1] As a result, no denomination has done more to support bivocational ministry than the Southern Baptist Convention. A number of state conventions have bivocational ministries specialists, such as Ray Guilder, who has that responsibility for the Tennessee Baptist Convention. The Kentucky Baptist Convention has assigned three men, David Aker, David Sandifer, and Charles Blair, to serve as field representatives to the bivocational ministers in that state. The SBC hosts an annual bivocational conference, and several regional events occur each year throughout the denomination to bring together bivocational ministers for fellowship, encouragement, and training.

One of the issues facing most denominations with bivocational ministers is how best to train these persons for ministry. Some SBC schools now offer specific training for persons interested in bivocational ministry. The Moench Center at Belmont University offers a bivocational certification program that does not require students to attend classes on site. Wayland Baptist University has a bivocational ministry specialization program in which students can take a business major or two minors along with a religion major. Campbellsville University has a Center for Bivocational Ministry that hosts training events for bivocational leadership.

The Tennessee Baptist Convention offers a certificate in bivocational ministry studies that can be earned by taking the skills courses offered by the Moench Center and some selected courses available through the Southern Baptist Convention's Seminary Extension program.

Ordination is not an issue for bivocational ministers in the SBC. Local churches, often with assistance from other association churches, have the responsibility to ordain pastors and other leaders in the church. The SBC has no educational requirements or other national standards that must be met prior to a minister's ordination being recognized throughout the denomination.

Despite the SBC's recognition of bivocational ministry, there are still some issues that need to be resolved. For twenty-one years the denomination had a national bivocational ministry consultant. Dale Holloway held that position until his retirement and was then replaced by Leon Wilson. However, when Wilson retired in 2003, the North American Mission Board (NAMB) decided not to fill the position. The Southern Baptist Bivocational Ministers Association recently unanimously voted to request that an office of bivocational ministry be funded by the denomination, but the NAMB has indicated that it has no plans to do so at this time.[2]

Both Holloway and Wilson published *The Bivocational Beacon* as a communication tool for the bivocational ministers in the SBC. This newsletter included articles designed to support and encourage bivocational ministers and to keep them informed of upcoming national and regional meetings. This publication has been eliminated, removing an important resource for the thousands of bivocational ministers in the denomination.

These two issues represent a significant reversal in support for SBC bivocational ministers, but there is still no denomination doing more to identify, train, and utilize bivocational ministers. Denominations serious about using this form of ministry would do well to closely examine the resources and affirmation the SBC has provided their bivocational ministers.

Evangelical Lutheran Church in America (ELCA)

Prior to 2000 few bivocational ministers were found in the Evangelical Lutheran Church in America even though the denomination struggled to find sufficient pastors for their small churches. In that year a report was issued titled *Ministry Needs and Resources in the 21st Century*.[3] Primarily written by Craig Settlage, director of Rostered and Authorized Ministry for the ELCA, this report found that there was no clergy shortage as believed by many within the denomination, but that it was becoming increasingly difficult to find pastoral leadership willing to serve in small churches. To compound this problem, as in many denominations, the number of small, financially struggling congregations was increasing in the ELCA. Moreover, the denomination had plans to develop two thousand new congregations by 2030. One of the recommendations in the report was that the denomination needed to use more bivocational ministers, and this recommendation has been implemented.

The ELCA has specific guidelines for persons in "shared-time ministry," which includes bivocational ministers. One of the interesting guidelines is that shared-time ministers are called by the synod rather than directly by a congregation. Settlage explained that this is to protect the pastor by ensuring that the job expectations and compensation are fair to the individual and fall within acceptable guidelines determined by the synod.[4] The ELCA does grant full ordination status to their bivocational ministers even if they have not completed seminary. The denomination has developed an alternative training program for clergy called Theological Education for Emerging Ministries (TEEM), which a number of bivocational ministers are using for their ministry training.

Because Settlage believes the ELCA will see a growing need for bivocational ministers, his office is taking specific steps to encourage persons to consider the possibility of their being called to this ministry. As students enter ELCA seminaries, they are challenged to consider that God may be calling them to a bivocational ministry, and dual-degree programs are being offered in these schools. Bishops are also encouraged to become more proactive in calling bivocational persons to serve churches within their synods.

The ELCA is no different than most denominations that are moving toward the use of more bivocational ministers. Sometimes fully funded pastors find it difficult to accept bivocational ministry as valid as fully funded ministry, but Settlage reports that as their bivocational ministers continue to provide solid ministries to their churches, this problem is quickly resolving, and many fully funded ministers now recognize the bivocational ministers in the ELCA as peers and colleagues.

A greater problem is the reluctance of small churches to accept that conditions may have changed within their churches and that they can no longer be served by a fully funded minister. Even though these churches may recognize that they have declined, they still believe they should have the services of a fully funded minister. Moving to a bivocational status is very difficult for some of these churches.

Church of the Nazarene

Pastors of Nazarene churches were asked in the 1993 Quadrennial Church Census of Nazarene congregations if they were bivocational. Thirty-one percent responded that they were bivocational either because they needed the extra income or because they felt their other career made their ministry more effective.[5] A 2005 study of Nazarene churches reported that 71 percent of their pastors were full-time without any other employment.[6] However, the study also indicated that churches with fewer than fifty in attendance were a little underrepresented, so the implication is that the number of bivocational ministers has remained somewhat steady during that twelve-year period. These numbers remain very similar to those reported by other denominations.

Mike Stipp, pastoral services coordinator for the Church of the Nazarene, says that anyone who feels called of God to a preaching ministry may be ordained once he or she has completed a validated course of study and been a district-licensed minister for at least three years.[7] Throughout this process the candidate will be interviewed annually by the district credentialing board and must be recommended for ordination by that board. Although their manual does not use the term *bivocational*, it does mention part-time ministers who may be ordained.

Similar to other denominations, small Nazarene churches are the most likely to be without a pastor. At the end of 2001, 80 percent of the pastoral vacancies in this denomination were in congregations averaging one hundred or fewer people.[8] Kenneth E. Crow of the Research Center of the Church of the Nazarene estimates that the denomination probably needs one thousand to two thousand bivocational ministers to achieve their mission in the United States.[9]

Presbyterian Church (USA) (PCUSA)

Like other denominations in the United States, the Presbyterian Church (USA) is made up primarily of small churches. The median size of their churches is 109. They suggest that a church needs 150 members to have a fully funded pastor with a part-time assistant, which means that two-thirds of their churches cannot afford a fully funded pastor.[10] The PCUSA is addressing this need through yoked churches and commissioned lay pastors and by developing ways to make bivocational ministry a more viable option for their churches.[11]

Some PCUSA schools offer creative educational opportunities for bivocational ministers. McCormick Theological Seminary in Chicago offers educational opportunities that are appealing to bivocational leaders. A number of their core classes are offered during the evenings, and the school offers a dual competency program that allows students to earn both a master of divinity and a master of social work. This can lead to employment and ministry opportunities that would be a good combination for a bivocational minister. Union Theological Seminary and Presbyterian School of Christian Education in Richmond, Virginia, has a doctor of ministry track specifically designed for leaders of small churches. Pastors of churches with fewer than 150 members are not charged any tuition to enroll in this program, and two of the courses are specifically oriented to small church ministry.

In addition to addressing the training needs of bivocational leadership, the PCUSA is also looking at how they attempt to match ministers and small churches. David Ezekiel, associate executive presbyter for congregational development in the Presbytery of Chicago, recommends that churches and judicatories spend some time understanding the dynamics of each church and trying to find a pastor who would be a good fit for the specific church rather than just trying to find someone who can preach there on the weekends.[12]

This is an excellent point that is often overlooked by many judicatories of every denomination. Few would think of just recommending warm bodies to their larger churches. An attempt is usually made to identify the specific needs a larger church has for its next pastor and to appoint or recommend persons who would be a good match for that church. However, when a small church starts looking for its next pastor, the assessment stage is sometimes overlooked and the search merely focuses on who might live nearby and could provide a preaching ministry to the church. This may explain why some of these churches remain small and never really develop a more effective ministry.

As the PCUSA begins to use more bivocational ministers, it faces many of the same problems identified in other traditions. Churches are often reluctant to accept the leadership of a bivocational minister. They may remember their glory years when they were served not only by a fully funded pastor but by a staff of ministers, and it is very difficult for them to accept that their congregation has been in a long, steady decline and can no longer afford the services of a fully funded pastor.

Clergy are also often reluctant to accept a bivocational position. Although many racial ethnic (a PCUSA term) pastors with the master of divinity degree are bivocational, Euro-American male pastors ordinarily will not consider a bivocational ministry. Like the racial ethnic pastors, women pastors in the PCUSA are often found in bivocational leadership.[13] According to 2005 statistics, the PCUSA had 1,203 women serving as pastors or copastors of a church, and 735 of them were leading churches with a membership size of 150 or less.[14]

Emergent Church

The emergent church is a movement designed to take the gospel into the postmodern society in which we live. Many within this movement believe that current church structures make this difficult and merely seek to revise how ministry is done. Others, however, attract a great deal of opposition from evangelical and conservative Christians due to their attempts to seemingly revise Scripture. One of the primary leaders of the emergent church, Brian McLaren, wrote a book titled *A Generous Orthodoxy* in 2004 that attracted much criticism by those who felt that his orthodoxy was too generous. Critics accused McLaren of refusing to clearly address many theological issues and rejecting historic orthodoxy on many issues he did address. Even McLaren admits that critics often accuse him and others within the emergent church of pluralistic relativism, but he also insists that those critics may be wrong and that the way forward for the church is to move through pluralistic relativism into something better.[15]

Leaving the theological issues for others to resolve, my interest in the emergent church is how bivocational ministry might play a part in it. Rick Smyre is president of the Center for Communities of the Future and an elder in the Presbyterian Church. He writes of the church, "We are entering an age when no standard models exist, because of constant change. New principles of thinking and new structures of organization will emerge as research and development create new experiments, new pilot concepts, and new networks of collaboration."[16]

This sounds like an excellent description of the emerging church, because there is no one model of emerging churches. Some are large and some are small. They meet in cities, rural communities, and suburban areas. Some meet in storefronts, some gather in beautiful church buildings, and others meet in homes. I mentioned in chapter 4 about one that meets in a supermarket parking lot at 3:00 A.M. Each church meets whenever and wherever it works best for them.

Although not much information is available on bivocational ministry in the emergent church, it seems likely that many of these churches will have bivocational leadership. While larger emergent churches, such as Solomon's Porch, Mosaic, and Mars Hill, will be led by fully funded staff, many emergent churches will remain small and rely on bivocational and lay leadership. Much of this will be by design. These churches believe that their mission is to start new churches throughout the surrounding area to reach as many people as possible. Growth will occur through multiplying congregations, not by adding people to the church membership list. Such churches are unlikely to grow sufficiently large to support a fully funded minister.

Formal theological education will not be a requirement for these bivocational leaders. Having qualities such as vision and passion and gifts of leadership and teaching will be more valuable to bivocational emergent church leaders than the ability to read Greek and Hebrew. Much of their training will come through mentoring and coaching relationships developed with other emergent leaders.

Getting Started in Bivocational Ministry

As we have seen, many denominations recognize and value the work bivocational ministers provide to churches. One question I am frequently asked is how a person who feels led to this ministry can get started. The first place to start is to talk to your pastor about the requirements and opportunities that exist within your tradition. Your pastor may be able to answer that question or refer you to someone within the judicatory who can get you started.

Your area minister, association missionary, district superintendent, or other judicatory leader should be your next contact. Some traditions have formal procedures that must be followed before beginning a bivocational ministry while others do not, and these judicatory leaders can help you understand the steps you need to take. They will also know what churches are seeking pastors who might be a good fit for your gifts and experiences, and they may be willing to submit your résumé to these churches.

Be aware, however, that even in those traditions that use bivocational ministers, not every pastor and judicatory leader is open to such ministry. Some will not value your sense of call to this ministry, and their attitudes and words can easily discourage someone just starting out. I speak from experience. More people in church leadership criticized my sense of call to bivocational ministry than encouraged me when I first started out. I hope you remember my comment earlier in the book about how being stubborn can be an asset to a bivocational minister, because you may have to ignore the critics in order to pursue the ministry God has given you.

Because I am most familiar with Baptist churches, I will share how this process often works in the bivocational church. One of my responsibilities as an area resource minister is to assist churches in seeking pastoral leadership. Because Baptist churches are autonomous, some prefer not to contact judicatory leaders for such assistance, but many do. I meet with the search committees of these churches and try to assess what they are seeking in their next pastor. I then compare that with a list of persons I know who feel called to bivocational ministry. After comparing the abilities of these individuals with the needs of the church, I send the church a list of names, or résumés if I have them, of those I feel may be able to serve that church. Of course, at that point it is up to the church and minister to meet and determine if God is calling the minister to serve this church.

The problem is that my list of persons seeking bivocational ministry is always much shorter than the number of churches looking for such leadership. If I do not know someone is interested in doing bivocational ministry, I am not able to give his or her information to churches. That is why it is vital to contact your judicatory leadership.

As mentioned earlier, some traditions have much more formal procedures that must be followed to serve as a bivocational minister. Judicatory leaders can assist persons who wish to become ministers within those traditions. Nondenominational churches often find their pastors through networking and now through various Internet sites. In these churches it is essential that pastors know of your interest in serving as a bivocational minister so they can share your name with search committees who are seeking such leadership.

Recommended Resources

Anderson, Leith. *A Church for the 21st Century: Bringing Change to Your Church to Meet the Challenges of a Changing Society*. Minneapolis: Bethany House, 1992.

Kimball, Dan. *The Emerging Church: Vintage Christianity for New Generations*. Grand Rapids: Zondervan, 2003.

Klasson, Ron and John Koessler. *No Little Places: The Untapped Potential of the Small-Town Church*. Grand Rapids: Baker, 1996.

McLaren, Brian D. *The Church on the Other Side: Doing Ministry in the Postmodern Matrix*. Grand Rapids: Zondervan, 2000.

Stetzer, Ed, and David Putman. *Breaking the Missional Code: Your Church Can Become a Missionary in Your Community*. Nashville: Broadman & Holman, 2006.

CONCLUSION

For several years I believed that God was calling me to the ministry, but I didn't see how that could happen. I was married with a family and saw no way I could put my life on hold while I went to college and seminary to prepare for pastoral ministry. I was active in our church, but in the back of my mind, I knew that God had called me to something more. One day I became aware of bivocational ministry as an option, and soon afterward a neighbor told me that Hebron Baptist Church was seeking a pastor. Although the church was located in the same county in which I had lived for most of my life, I was not familiar with the church. Still, I felt led to send my résumé to the church, and a few months later the church called me to become their pastor.

The twenty-year period I served as the bivocational pastor of Hebron ranks as one of the most enjoyable times of my life. Although the work was not always easy, it was very rewarding, and I always believed I was making a difference. People in our congregation allowed me access into their lives at their most joyous and painful times. I truly was able to rejoice with those who rejoiced and to weep with those who wept. This was not the work of a CEO or the head of a religious organization; it was pastoral ministry in its purest form.

Bivocational ministry is true servant leadership. My role was very simple. I was there to serve the needs of the congregation, to lead them in following God's guidance, and to teach them the Scriptures that they might grow as disciples of the Lord Jesus Christ. We sometimes want to make pastoral ministry much more complicated than that, but bivocational ministry encourages a simpler ministry that is more shepherding than managing.

Throughout this book we have seen how the need for bivocational ministers is growing. There are not enough persons serving as bivocational ministers to meet the current need, much less the expanding bivocational opportunities that will present themselves in the future. This need for bivocational leadership has not caught God by surprise. The Lord has been calling men and women to serve as bivocational ministers, and you may be one of those persons. Perhaps, like me, you have resisted that call because you did not see how you could do it. But if God has called you to this ministry, it is because you have already been gifted for it, and God can open the doors and use you in a powerful way to touch the lives of a church and community in ways you could never imagine. God is only waiting for you to say yes to the call that is already there.

Many of you reading this book are now serving as bivocational ministers. My hope is that this book has been a blessing and encouragement to you. You may never receive the recognition that other ministers receive, but the Lord knows who you are and has noted the work you are doing. Isn't that the only thing that really matters? Bivocational ministers do not serve for the applause and recognition of the world, but for God's approval. We want to hear the Lord say, "Well done, good and faithful servant! You have been faithful with a few things; I will put you in charge of many things. Come and share your master's happiness!" (Matthew 25:21). As faithful bivocational ministers, we will one day hear these words if we keep seven things in mind.

1. *Never allow your ministry to take the place of your personal time with God.* We must continue to grow as disciples for our own spiritual fulfillment and because we cannot take our people further than we ourselves are going. Our work can threaten to rob us of our first love if we begin to focus on what we are doing for God rather than spending time each day enjoying an intimate

and growing relationship with the one who seeks such a relationship with us.

2. *Do not neglect your family for the sake of ministry.* If God has given you a family, you have also been given responsibility for the nurture of that family. Sacrificing family for ministry is a poor trade that does not honor God. It also provides a poor model for the families in your church. They need to see in their pastoral leadership a godly home that reflects the difference God can make in the home.

3. *Never lose your sense of calling to this ministry.* The enemy will try to sidetrack you from what the Lord has called you to do. There will be times when you may doubt or even question your call, but these are the times when it is even more important to draw closer to God. We sink only when we take our eyes off God. (see Matthew 14:30–31)

4. *Love your people as much as God does.* These are people for whom Jesus Christ gave his life, and they are special in God's eyes. Remind them regularly how much God loves them, and don't be afraid to tell them that you love them as well. It may be the most important thing you ever tell them.

5. *Continually seek a fresh vision from God for your church.* Not having God's vision has caused many churches to wander aimlessly, achieving little for the kingdom of God. A lack of vision is also one of the biggest contributors to conflict in the church. It wastes precious resources and has a negative impact on the church's testimony.

6. *Be a lifelong learner.* Our world is constantly changing, and unless we understand these changes, we will continue to offer ministries that do not have the same impact on people's live that they used to have. Invest in books, conferences, workshops, and any other training opportunities you find that may be helpful to your ministry.

7. *Don't do ministry alone.* This was one of my biggest mistakes earlier in my ministry. Find a coach, a mentor, or someone

who can walk with you in your ministry. This should be a person who will listen to you, pray for you, refuse to judge you, and ask questions that will help you find solutions to the ministry issues you will face.

May you clearly understand God's call on your life and pursue that call with passion and commitment. And may God's richest blessings be on all you do.

SERMON PLANNER

Date _____

Sermon Title _____

Sermon Text _____

Sermon Thesis _____

_____

Sermon Objective _____

Additional Supporting Texts   **Other Resources Used**

_____   _____

_____   _____

Main Points

_____

_____

_____

_____

_____

SERMON EVALUATION

Congregational Response

_____

_____

Personal Feelings about the Message

_____

_____

COMPENSATION WORKSHEET

Salary and Housing

    Cash Salary   _____

    Housing Allowance   _____

or

    Parsonage Rental Value   _____

    Utilities Allowance   _____

Benefits

    Medical and Dental Insurance   _____

    Social Security Offset   _____

    Retirement   _____

Reimbursement for Ministry-Related Expenses

    Book Allowance   _____

    Mileage at _____ per Mile   _____

    Continuing Education   _____

    Convention Expenses   _____

    Hospitality   _____

GOAL SETTING

Effective people know that goal setting is essential to making the best use of their resources and time. Some goals should be short-term (a month or so), some goals should take several months to a year to achieve, and some goals should be long-term (over a year). You should set goals in every area of importance in your life: God, family, ministry, work, and self-care. Each area should have at least one goal, but it is usually best not to have more than eight goals total. All goals must be written out, and each goal must be a SMART goal.

S pecific
M easurable
A chievable
R elevant
T ime-defined

When setting each goal, you need to answer the following questions:
• What is my goal?

• How will achieving this goal affect my life or the lives of others?

• What might keep me from achieving this goal?

• Who can help me to achieve this goal?

• Are there new skills I need to learn in order to achieve this goal?

• What are the steps I need to take to achieve this goal?

• By what date do I want to achieve this goal?

NOTES

INTRODUCTION

1. Patricia M. Y. Chang, "Assessing the Clergy Supply in the 21st Century," *Pulpit and Pew: Research on Pastoral Leadership*, 2004, http://www.pulpit andpew.duke.edu/chang.html.

2. An initiative of The Ministers Council ABCUSA in partnership with that denomination's National Ministries, BivoNet is designed to provide resources, encouragement, and assistance for our bivocational ministers. The latest issue of its e-newsletter, *Vital Churches*, can be viewed online at www.ministerscoun cil.com/periodicals.

3. Unlike counselors and therapists, who typically aid individuals with diagnosable physical, emotional, or psychological challenges, life coaches "work with emotionally healthy people who are looking to make changes in their lives to become or achieve more" (http://www.christiancoaches.com/faq.html, accessed January 12, 2007.)

CHAPTER 1

1. Ron Crandall, *Turnaround Strategies for the Small Church*, Effective Church Series, ed. Herb Miller (Nashville: Abingdon, 1995), 42.

2. Dennis Bickers, *The Bivocational Pastor: Two Jobs, One Ministry* (Kansas City, MO: Beacon Hill, 2004).

3. Dennis Bickers, *The Healthy Small Church: Diagnosis and Treatment for the Big Issues* (Kansas City, MO: Beacon Hill, 2005), 128–33.

4. Doran C. McCarty, *Meeting the Challenge of Bivocational Ministry: A Bivocational Reader* (Nashville: Seminary Extension, 1996), 201–02.

CHAPTER 2

1. William Barclay, *The Acts of the Apostles*, rev. ed, The Daily Study Bible Series (Philadelphia: Westminster, 1976), 135.

2. Luther M. Dorr, *The Bivocational Pastor* (Nashville: Broadman, 1988), 24.

3. Reported by the Association of Presbyterian Tentmakers, http://www.pc usa.org/oga/affinity05/aptentmakers.pdf (accessed March 2, 2007).

4. Doran C. McCarty, *Meeting the Challenge of Bivocational Ministry: A Bivocational Reader* (Nashville: Seminary Extension, 1996), 16.

5. Becky R. McMillan and Matthew J. Price, "How Much Should We Pay the Pastor? A Fresh Look at Clergy Salaries in the 21st Century," *Pulpit and Pew: Research on Pastoral Leadership*, 2003, http://www.pulpitand pew.duke.edu/salarystudy.pdf.

6. Lyle E. Schaller, *Small Congregation, Big Potential: Ministry in the Small Membership Church* (Nashville: Abingdon, 2003), 24.

7. Lyle E. Schaller, *Innovations in Ministry: Models for the 21st Century* (Nashville: Abingdon, 1994), 21.

8. Schaller, *Small Congregation, Big Potential*, 60.

9. Ed Stetzer, *Planting Missional Churches: Planting a Church That's Biblically Sound and Reaching People in Culture* (Nashville: Broadman & Holman, 2006), 226.

10. Ibid., 227.

11. George Barna, *Revolution* (Wheaton: Tyndale, 2005), 13.

12. Ibid., 105.

CHAPTER 3

1. Reported at a bivocational ministers' conference in Louisville, KY, April 1, 2006.

2. Deborah A. Bruce, "Tentmakers: Combining Calls and Careers," Research Services Presbyterian Church (U.S.A.), Louisville, KY, http://www.pc usa.org/research/Monday/tentmkr.htm (accessed March 2, 2007).

3. L. Ronald Brushwyler, "Bi-Vocational Pastors: A Research Report," The Midwest Ministry Development Service, Westchester, IL, 3, http://www.mid westministry.org/bi-voc.html (accessed June 24, 2006).

4. Ibid., 12.

5. Ibid., 5.

6. Bruce, "Tentmakers," 1.

CHAPTER 4

1. Ron Blake, "Pastoral/Congregational Care in the 21st Century," *The Pastor's Guide to Effective Ministry* (Kansas City, MO: Beacon Hill, 2002), 105.

2. Michael J. Quicke, *360-Degree Preaching: Hearing, Speaking, and Living the Word* (Grand Rapids: Baker, 2003), 121.

3. George Barna, *The Power of Team Leadership: Finding Strength in Shared Responsibility* (Colorado Springs: Water-Brook, 2001), 21.

4. Neil Cole, *Organic Church: Growing Faith Where Life Happens* (San Francisco: Jossey-Bass, 2005), 14.

CHAPTER 5

1. Dennis W. Bickers, *The Tentmaking Pastor: The Joy of Bivocational Ministry* (Grand Rapids: Baker, 2000), and *The Bivocational Pastor: Two Jobs, One Ministry* (Kansas City, MO: Beacon Hill, 2004).

2. Http://www.drphil.com/articles/article/131 (accessed March 2, 2007).

3. H. B. London Jr. and Neil B. Wiseman, *The Heart of a Great Pastor: How to Grow Strong and Thrive Wherever God Has Planted You* (Ventura, CA.: Regal, 1994), 20.

CHAPTER 6

1. I cover the benefits of long pastorates and the problems generated by a series of short pastorates in greater detail in my two previous books on bivocational ministry: *The Tentmaking Pastor: The Joy of Bivocational Ministry* (Grand Rapids, Baker, 2000), and *The Bivocational Pastor: Two Jobs, One Ministry* (Kansas City, MO: Beacon Hill, 2004).

2. Cindy Kerr, "Small churches offer intimacy, ownership and involvement," *BP News*, November 10, 1998, http://www.sbcbaptistpress.org/bpnews.asp?ID=4934 (accessed July 8, 2006).

3. Richard A. Harris, "Bi-Vocational Church Planting," http://www.urban impact.netforms.com/bivoc.html (accessed March 2, 2007).

CHAPTER 7

1. Richard A. Swenson, *Margin: Restoring Emotional, Physical, Financial, and Time Reserves to Overloaded Lives* (Colorado Springs: NavPress, 1992), 227.

2. Aubrey Malphurs, *Strategic Planning: A New Model for Church and Ministry Leaders* (Grand Rapids: Baker, 1999).

3. John Maxwell, *Partners in Prayer: Support and Strengthen Your Pastor and Church Leaders* (Nashville: Nelson, 1996), 2–3.

4. Dennis Bickers, *The Healthy Small Church: Diagnosis and Treatment for the Big Issues* (Kansas City, MO: Beacon Hill, 2005), 130–31.

5. Jill M. Hudson, *When Better Isn't Enough: Evaluation Tools for the 21st-Century Church* (Herndon, VA: Alban Institute, 2004), 155–59.

CHAPTER 8

1. Linda Lawson, "'Tentmaking' ministers predicted to become Southern Baptist norm," *BP News*, August 11, 1999, http://www.bpnews.net/printer friendly.asp?ID=373 (accessed August 20, 2006).

2. Connie Davis Bushey and William Perkins, "Bivocational ministers ask NAMB for office to support their work," *BP News*, June 7, 2006, http://www.bpnews.net/printerfriendly.asp?ID=23417 (accessed August 21, 2006).

3. A. Craig Settlage, *Ministry Needs and Resources in the 21st Century* (Chicago: Evangelical Lutheran Church in America, 2000), 8.

4. From a telephone conversation with the author on August 16, 2006.

5. Kenneth E. Crow, "Recognizing, Equipping, and Sustaining the People God Is Calling to Pastor Smaller Churches," Church of the Nazarene Research Center, May 30, 2002, 8.

6. Kenneth E. Crow, "Faith Communities Today 2005," Church of the Nazarene Research Center, June 2006, 7.

7. In an e-mail to the author from Mike Stipp dated August 20, 2006.

8. Crow, "Recognizing, Equipping, and Sustaining," 5.

9. Ibid., 3.

10. David Ezekiel, *Tentmaking—From a Congregational Development*

Perspective, speech given to the 2005 National Conference on Tentmaking/Bi-Vocational Ministry on November 5, 2005, http://www.nassam.org/images/2005 Conference-Ezekiel.pdf (accessed August 28, 2006).

11. Http://www.pcusa.org/ga217/delegates/commissionersquestions.pdf (accessed August 28, 2006).

12. Ezekiel, *Tentmaking*, 2.

13. Http://www.pcusa.org/ministers/pdf/notes/recruitmentsupport.pdf (accessed August 28, 2006).

14. Http://www.pcusa.org/research/compstats/cs2005/2005_table15.pdf (accessed August 29, 2006).

15. Brian D. McLaren, *A Generous Orthodoxy* (Grand Rapids: Zondervan, 2004), 287.

16. Rick Smyre, "Building Capacities for Community and Church Transformation," *Net Results*, July–August 2006, 6.